Shortcut to
Spanish

The 100 Words You Need to Speak
over 500 Spanish Phrases

Berlitz Publishing
New York   Munich   Singapore

Contacting the Editors
Every effort has been made to provide accurate information in this publication, but changes are inevitable. The publisher cannot be responsible for any resulting loss, inconvenience or injury. We would appreciate it if readers would call our attention to any errors or outdated information by contacting Berlitz Publishing, 193 Morris Avenue, Springfield, NJ 07081, USA.
email: comments@berlitzbooks.com

First Printing: February 2006

Printed in China

Cover photo © BananaStock Ltd.

Author: Christina Sanchez

Illustrations: Katrin Merle

Editorial: Maria Amparo Pérez Roch, Emily Bernath, Christopher Gross, Christiane Heil, Juergen Lorenz

Production: Elizabeth Gaynor, Blair Swick

Satisfaction guaranteed—If you are dissatisfied with this product for any reason, send the complete package, your dated sales receipt showing price and store name, and a brief note describing your dissatisfaction to: Berlitz Publishing, Langenscheidt Publishing Group, Dept. L, 36-36 33rd St., Long Island City, NY 11106. You'll receive a full refund.

Contents

How to Use This Book

You need only to memorize 100 Spanish words in order to speak over 500 of the most useful phrases. To take full advantage of this concept please follow these simple steps:

- Memorize the vocabulary in the **100 Words section** in the beginning of the book. The words have been organized in groups to make it easier for you to memorize them. You'll notice that the verbs listed in the 100 Words section aren't fully conjugated. You'll need only the verb forms listed in this book to make 500+ phrases.

- You memorize only 100 words but your basic vocabulary actually consists of more since you are able to create compound words. The important ones are also listed in the **100 Words section**, others will be explained in tip boxes or footnotes. LA indicates Latin-American variations. The abbreviation for singular is *sing.*, for plural *pl.*, for formal *form.* and informal *inform.* Masculine forms are indicated by ♂, feminine forms by ♀.

- The **100 Words section** as well as each individual chapter contain **Language Tip** boxes in red explaining important rules with examples.

- **Country and Culture Tips**, in green, inform you about important customs and traditions in Spanish-speaking countries.

- The Chapters are organized by topics, e.g. Accommodations. Each chapter provides you with the basic and most useful expressions to function in a variety of situations. At times, phrases are supplemented by illustrations.

- The **Dictionary** in the back of the book gives you all the Spanish words and expressions used in this program.

- The phonetic system used in this book makes it easy to pronounce the Spanish words. Simply read the words as you would read them in English.

Pronunciation

There are variations between the Spanish spoken in Spain and that in the Americas – although each is understood by the other.

Consonants

Letter	Approximate Pronunciation	Example
b	1. as in English 2. between vowels as in English, but softer	**bueno** **bebida**
c	1. before **e** and **i**, like *th* in *thin*; in Latin America, like *s* in *sit* 2. otherwise like *k* in *kit*	**centro** **como**
ch	as in English	**mucho**
d	1. as in English *dog*, but less decisive 2. between vowels and at the end of a word, like *th* in *this* (only in Spain)	**dónde** **usted**
g	1. before **e** and **i**, like *ch* in Scottish *loch* 2. otherwise, like *g* in *get*	**urgente** **ninguno**
h	always silent	**hombre**
j	like *ch* in Scottish *loch*	**bajo**
ll	like *lli* in *million*	**lleno**
ñ	like *ni* in *onion*	**señor**
qu	like *k* in *kick*	**quince**
r	more strongly trilled (like a Scottish *r*), especially at the beginning of a word	**río**
rr	strongly trilled	**arriba**
s	1. like *s* in *same* 2. before **b, d, g, l, m, n**, like *s* in *rose*	**vista** **mismo**

v	like *b* in *bad*, but softer	**viejo**
z	like *th* in *thin*	**brazo**
	in Latin America, like *s* in *sit*	

Letters **f, k, l, m, n, p, t, x** and **y** are pronounced as in English.

Vowels

a	in length, between *a* in English *pat*, and *a* in English *bar*	**gracias**
e	1. like *e* in *get* 2. in a syllable ending in a vowel like *e* in *they*	**puedo** **me**
i	like *ee* in *feet*	**sí**
o	like *o* in *got*	**dos**
u	1. like *oo* in *food* 2. silent after *g* in words like **guerra**, **guiso**, except where marked ü, as in **antigüedad**	**una**
y	a vowel only when alone at the end of a word, like *ee* in *feet*	**y**

In words ending with a vowel, **-n** or **-s**, the next to last syllable is stressed, e.g. **ma<u>ña</u>na**; in words ending in a consonant, the last syllable is stressed, e.g. **se<u>ñor</u>**; the acute accent (´) is used in Spanish to indicate a syllable is stressed, not a change in sound, e.g. **r<u>í</u>o**.

Some Spanish words have more than one meaning; the accent mark is employed to distinguish between them, e.g. **él** (he) and **el** (the); **sí** (yes) and **si** (if); **tú** (you) and **tu** (your).

100 Words

1	**sí** see	yes
2	**no** no	no; not; no one; none
3	**el** ♂ ehl	the
	la ♀ lah	the
	los ♂ *pl.* lohs	the *pl.*; they
	las ♀ *pl.* lahs	the *pl.*; they
4	**un** ♂ oon	a/an
	una ♀ <u>oo</u>nah	a/an
5	**este** <u>ehs</u>teh	this
	estos ♂ *pl.* <u>ehs</u>tos	these
	esta ♀ <u>ehs</u>tah	this one
	estas ♀ *pl.* <u>ehs</u>tahs	these
	esto ♂ <u>ehs</u>to	this here; that there

Language Tip

The Spanish language has two genders: masculine and feminine. The male definite article is *el* and the female *la*. The plural versions of these articles are *los* and *las*.
The pronouns *esto(s)* and *esta(s)* (this/these, masculine and feminine) simply have the letter -s added for the plural form.

6	**yo** yo	I
7	**me** meh	me
8	**mi** mee	my; mine
9	**tu** too	you/your *sing. inform.*

10 **te** teh	(to/for) you/your *sing. inform.*
11 **lo** lo	him/her/it
12 **le** leh	(to/for) him/her/it/you *form.*
13 **usted** oos<u>tehd</u>	you *sing. form.*
14 **su** soo	his/her/its; their; your *sing. form.*
15 **se** seh	one(self); you
16 **nos** nos	us
17 **en** ehn	in
18 **de** deh	from; (out) of
19 **a** ah	to
20 **con** kon	with
21 **hasta** <u>ahs</u>tah	until
22 **para** <u>pah</u>rah	for; in order to
23 **por** por	for; while; during
24 **y** ee	and

Language Tip

Por means "for" in clauses such as: *Gracias por todo* (Thanks for everything). When used with expressions of time it means "while/during": *por la mañana* (during/in the morning). In connection with *aquí / acá*, "here", as in *por aquí / acá*, it can mean "right here (nearby)" or "this way". Used in combination with *dónde*, "where", (*por dónde*) it means "which way".

25	**pero** <u>peh</u>ro	but
26	**muy** mwee	very
27	**algo** <u>ahl</u>go	something
28	**nada** <u>na</u>hdah **de nada** deh <u>na</u>hdah	nothing you're welcome
29	**otro** <u>o</u>tro	another; one more
30	**poco** <u>po</u>ko	(a) little
31	**menos** <u>meh</u>nos	less
32	**mucho** <u>moo</u>cho	much
33	**más** mahs	more
34	**demasiado** dehmahsee<u>yah</u>-doh	too much
35	**todo** <u>to</u>do	all; everything
36	**uno** <u>oo</u>no	one
37	**dos** dos	two
38	**quién** kee<u>yehn</u>	who
39	**qué** keh	what; Which one? How ...!

Language Tip

The female forms and the plural forms of *mucho*, *todo* and *otro* change endings in the same way as most Spanish adjectives. For the female version of *mucho*, simply replace the *-o* at the end with an *-a* to obtain *mucha*. To form the plural, add *-s* to the respective form to obtain *muchos* (♂ *pl.*) and *muchas* (♀ *pl.*).

40	**que** keh	as; what; this/that *relative pronoun*; which *relative pronoun*
41	**cuándo** <u>kwahn</u>do	when
42	**cuánto** <u>kwahn</u>to **cuántos** <u>kwahn</u>tos	how much how many
43	**dónde** <u>don</u>deh	where
44	**cómo** <u>ko</u>mo	how
45	**hoy** oyee	today
46	**mañana** mahn<u>yah</u>-nah	tomorrow
47	**ya** yah	already
48	**luego** <u>lweh</u>go	afterwards; later
49	**tarde** <u>tah</u>rdeh	late
50	**también** tahmbee<u>yehn</u>	also; too
51	**aquí (LA: acá)** ah<u>kee</u> (LA ah<u>kah</u>)	here
52	**cerca** <u>sehr</u>kah	nearby
53	**el día** ehl <u>dee</u>-ah	day
54	**la mañana** lah mahn<u>yah</u>nah	morning
55	**la tarde** lah <u>tah</u>rdeh	afternoon; evening
56	**la noche** lah <u>no</u>cheh	(late) evening; night
57	**el año** ehl <u>ah</u>nyo	year

58 **el tiempo** ehl teeyehm-po   time; weather

59 **la cama** lah kahmah   bed

60 **la habitación**
lah ahbeetah-seeyon   room

61 **el calor** ehl kahlor   warmth; heat

62 **el regalo** ehl reh-ghahlo   gift; present

63 **el favor** ehl fahbor   favor
    por favor por fahbor   please

Language Tip

The plural for Spanish nouns ending in -o, -a or -e is formed by adding -s: *regalo* – *regalos*; *día* – *días*; *tarde* – *tardes*.
If the Spanish noun ends with a consonant, such as *l*, *n*, *r*, *z*, etc., the plural is formed by adding -es: e.g. *habitación* – *habitaciones*.
As a general rule, most nouns ending in -o are masculine, while nouns ending in -a are usually feminine.

---

64 **bueno** bwehno   good

65 **mejor** mehkhor   better

66 **bien** beeyehn   good *adverb*

67 **mal** mahl   bad; poorly
            adverb

68 **bonito** boneeto   nice; beautiful

69 **grande** grahndeh   big; large; great

Language Tip

In Spanish, adjectives always agree in gender (masculine or feminine) and number (singular or plural) with the noun they modify:

El regalo es bonito (The present is beautiful).
La cama es bonita (The bed is beautiful).
Los regalos son bonitos (The presents are beautiful).

To describe a verb, use *bien* (well) instead of *bueno*: *Estoy bien* (I'm well).

70 **ser** sehr		to be
soy soyee		I am
eres <u>eh</u>rehs		you are *sing. inform.*
es ehs		he/she/it is;
		you are *sing. form.*
somos <u>so</u>mos		we are
son son		they are
71 **estar** eh<u>stahr</u>		to be
estoy eh<u>stoy</u>ee		I am
estás eh<u>stahs</u>		you are *sing. inform.*
está eh<u>stah</u>		he/she/it is;
		you are *sing. form.*
estamos eh<u>stah</u>mos		we are

For usage of **ser** and **estar** see Language Tip on page 14.

Language Tip

The Spanish verbs *ser* and *estar* are both translated as "to be". While *ser* refers to a permanent condition, *estar* is used to describe a present status, one that might change. Consequently, one says: *Juanita es muy guapa* (Juanita is very pretty), but *Juanita está muy guapa esta noche* (Juanita is very pretty tonight).

72 **hacer** ahsehr — to do; to make
   hago ahgo — I do
   haces ahsehs — you do *sing. inform.*
   hace ahseh — he/she/it does; you do *sing. form.*

   hacemos ahsehmos — we do

73 **poder** podehr — can; to be able to
   puedo pwehdo — I can
   podría podree-ah — I could; he/she/it could; you could *sing. form.*

   puedes pweh-dehs — you can *sing. inform.*
   podrías podree-ahs — you could *sing. inform.*
   puede pweh-deh — he/she/it can; you can *sing. form.*

   podemos podehmos — we can

74 **querer** kehrehr — to like; to want; to love
   quiero keeyeh-ro — I want
   quieres keeyeh-rehs — you want *sing. inform.*
   quiere keeyeh-reh — he/she/it wants; you want *sing. form.*

   queremos kehrehmos — we want

75 **tener** teh<u>neh</u>r   to have
   tengo <u>teh</u>ngo   I have
   tienes teey<u>eh</u>-nehs   you have *sing. inform.*
   tiene teey<u>eh</u>-neh   he/she/it has;
       you have *sing. form.*

   tenemos teh<u>neh</u>mos   we have

Language Tip

Together with *que* the verb *tener* means "must": *Tengo que comer algo* (I must eat something).

---

76 **necesito** nehseh<u>see</u>-to   I need (to)
   necesitamos   we need (to)
   nehsehsee-<u>tah</u>mos

77 **ir** eer   to go, drive
   voy boyee   I go
   vas bahs   you go *sing. inform.*
   va bahs   he/she/it goes;
       you go *sing. form.*

   vamos <u>bah</u>mos   we go

Language Tip

The meaning of *ir* is "to go". Together with *a* and another verb in the infinitive it can also be used to speak about something in the future: *Voy a comer algo* (I will eat something).

---

78 **comer** ko<u>meh</u>r   to eat
   come <u>ko</u>meh   he/she/it eats;
       you eat *sing. form.*

79	**ver** behr	to see; to meet
	veo <u>beh</u>-oh	I see
	ves behs	you see *sing. inform.*
	vemos <u>beh</u>mos	we see
80	**vivir** bee<u>beer</u>	to live
	vivo <u>bee</u>bo	I live
	vives <u>bee</u>behs	you live *sing. inform.*
	vive <u>bee</u>beh	he/she/it lives; you live *sing. form.*
	vivimos bee<u>bee</u>mos	we live
81	**me llamo** meh <u>yah</u>mo	I'm called; my name is
	te llamas teh <u>yah</u>mahs	you are called *sing. inform.*
	se llama seh <u>yah</u>mah	he/she/it is called; you are called *sing. form.*
82	**comprar** kom<u>prahr</u>	to buy
	compro <u>kom</u>pro	I buy
83	**gusta** <u>goos</u>tah	he/she/it likes
	gustas <u>goos</u>tahs	you like *sing. inform.*
	gustaría goostah<u>ree</u>-ah	he/she/it would like you would like *sing. form.*
84	**entrar** ehn<u>trahr</u>	to enter
85	**pagar** pah<u>gahr</u>	to pay
86	**ayudar** ah-yoo<u>dahr</u>	to help
87	**beber** beh<u>behr</u>	to drink
88	**dormir** dor<u>meer</u>	to sleep
89	**cuesta** <u>kwehs</u>-tah	it costs
	cuestan <u>kwehs</u>-tahn	they cost
90	**duele** <u>dweh</u>leh	it hurts

91 **hay** eye — there is; there are
   hay que eye keh — one has to

92 **he** eh — I am; I have
   auxiliary verb for the past
   hemos ehmos — we are; we have

93 **perdido** pehrdee-do — lost; confused

94 **roto** roto — broken; torn

95 **estado** ehstahdo — have been

Language Tip

The auxiliary verbs *he/hemos* and such adjectives as *perdido* (lost), *roto* (broken) or verb forms like *estado* (have been) allow you to speak in the past tense: *He roto…* means "I broke/damaged … ".

---

96 **Hola.** olah — Hello.

97 **Adiós.** ahdeeyos — Good-bye.

98 **Gracias.** grah-seeyahs — Thanks.

99 **Perdón.** pehrdon — Excuse me.

100 **Estados Unidos de América**
    ehstahdos oonee-dos — United States of America
    Gran Bretaña
    grahn breh-tahnyah — Great Britain
    Canada
    kahnahdah — Canada

Meeting People

Greetings

The following greetings can be used during the day as well as in the evening or at night. You can use them for both informal and formal address:

Hola. <u>o</u>lah

Hello./Good day/ morning/evening.

Hola a todos.
<u>o</u>lah ah <u>to</u>dos

Hello everyone.

Hola a todas. ♀
<u>o</u>lah ah <u>to</u>dahs

Hello everyone.

Language Tip

The masculine form of *todos* ("all", here meaning "everyone") is used when addressing all-male or mixed-gender groups. The feminine form, *todas,* is used only when speaking to an all-female group.

You could also be more precise and say:

Buenos días. <u>bweh</u>nos <u>dee</u>ahs

Good morning/good day.

Buenas tardes.
<u>bweh</u>nahs <u>tahr</u>dehs

Good day/good evening.

Buenas noches.
<u>bweh</u>nahs <u>no</u>chehs

Good night.

Culture Tip

In Spain and Latin America, the salutation *buenos días* can be heard from the early morning through lunchtime. After lunch, the appropriate greeting is *buenas tardes.* Later in the evening or before going to bed, you would say *buenas noches.*

In addition to a verbal greeting, many people greet each other with a peck on either cheek. In much of Latin America, young men will gently hit fists, and sometimes hug, rather than exchange kisses as a greeting.

Saying Good-bye

There are different ways to say good-bye:

Adiós. ahdee<u>yos</u>　　　　　　　Good-bye / Bye.

Adiós a todos.　　　　　　　　Good-bye everyone.
ahdee<u>yos</u> ah <u>to</u>dos

Adiós a todas. ♀　　　　　　　Good-bye everyone.
ahdee<u>yos</u> ah <u>to</u>dahs

Hasta luego. <u>ah</u>stah <u>lweh</u>go　　See you later.

Adiós, hasta luego.　　　　　　Bye, see you later.
ahdee<u>yos</u> <u>ah</u>stah <u>lweh</u>go

¡Nos vemos! nos <u>beh</u>mos　　　So long!

Language Tip

In Spanish, exclamation clauses start with an exclamation mark that is turned upside down. Questions start with a question mark that is also turned upside down.

If you want to be more precise when departing, say:

¡Hasta mañana!
<u>ah</u>stah mahn<u>ya</u>hnah

Until tomorrow!

¡Hasta esta tarde!
<u>ah</u>stah <u>eh</u>stah <u>tah</u>rdeh

Until this afternoon/evening!

¡Hasta esta noche!
<u>ah</u>stah <u>eh</u>stah <u>no</u>cheh

Until this evening/tonight!

¡Hasta mañana por la tarde!
<u>ah</u>stah mahn<u>ya</u>hnah por lah <u>tah</u>rdeh

Until tomorrow afternoon/evening!

¡Hasta mañana por la noche!
<u>ah</u>stah mahn<u>ya</u>hnah por lah <u>no</u>cheh

Until tomorrow evening/night!

¡Hasta la una! <u>ah</u>stah lah <u>oo</u>nah

Until one o'clock!

¡Hasta las dos! <u>ah</u>stah lahs dos

Until two o'clock!

¡Hasta las … [time]! <u>ah</u>stah lahs

Until …!

See page 109 for numbers.

¡Hasta mañana a la una!
<u>ah</u>stah mahn<u>ya</u>hnah ah lah <u>oo</u>nah

Until tomorrow at one!

¡Hasta mañana a las dos de la tarde! <u>ah</u>stah mahn<u>ya</u>hnah ah lahs dos deh lah <u>tah</u>rdeh

Until tomorrow afternoon at two!

¡Hasta el …! <u>ah</u>stah ehl

Until …!

See page 111 for days of the week.

Culture Tip

Spaniards and Latinos love to go out at night and often party until the early hours of the morning. Especially in Spain, nightlife really takes off well after midnight, so if you want to join in, taking an afternoon nap, a *siesta*, is highly recommended. Such midday rest also takes into account the sweltering afternoon heat felt in the country in the summer months.

A last farewell greeting to close with:

¡Todo lo mejor!*   All the best!
<u>to</u>do lo meh<u>khor</u>

¡Buen día! bwehn <u>dee</u>ah   Have a nice day!

Language Tip

If the adjective *bueno* (good) is positioned in front of (not behind) a noun, the vowel *-o* at the end is dropped as in the following examples: *buen día* (nice day) or *buen tiempo* (nice weather).

---

* Idiomatic expression:
   ¡Todo lo mejor! todo lo meh<u>khor</u>   All the best!

Introductions

If you want to find out the name of the person you are talking to:

¿Cómo te llamas?
<u>ko</u>mo teh <u>yah</u>mahs

What's your name?
sing. inform.

¿Cómo se llama usted?
<u>ko</u>mo seh <u>yah</u>mah oos<u>teh</u>d

What is your name?
sing. form.

To reply when asked for your own name and when introducing yourself and others:

Yo soy ... yo soyee

I am/my name is ...

Soy ... soyee

I am/my name is ...

Me llamo ... meh <u>yah</u>mo

My name is ...

Este es ... [name]. ♂
<u>ehs</u>teh ehs

This is ...

Esta es ... [name]. ♀
<u>ehs</u>tah ehs

This is ...

Language Tip

Spanish regularly drops the personal pronoun, unless one uses it for emphasis, contrast or to avoid confusion. Though it is possible to introduce yourself with *Yo soy ...* (I am ...) you would normally just say *Soy ...*

Saying Thanks and Paying Compliments

When away on vacation there are many situations in which you will want to say thanks:

Gracias. <u>grah</u>-seeyahs
Thanks.

Muchas gracias.
<u>mooch</u>ahs <u>grah</u>-seeyahs
Many thanks.

The appropriate reply would be:

De nada. deh <u>nah</u>dah
You're welcome.

If you want to to be more precise you could say:

Muchas gracias por ...
<u>mooch</u>ahs <u>grah</u>-seeyahs por
Many thanks for ...

el café
ehl kah<u>feh</u>

la cerveza
lah cer<u>veh</u>zah

el vino
ehl <u>vee</u>no

Muchas gracias por todo.
<u>mooch</u>ahs <u>grah</u>-seeyahs por <u>to</u>do
Many thanks for everything.

Muchas gracias por todo esto.
<u>mooch</u>ahs <u>grah</u>-seeyahs por <u>to</u>do <u>ehs</u>to
Many thanks for all that.

Gracias a todos.
<u>grah</u>-seeyahs ah <u>to</u>dos
Thank you all.

Muchas gracias a todas. ♀
moochahs grah-seeyahs ah todahs

Many thanks to all of you.

Gracias por tu regalo.
grah-seeyahs por too reh-ghahlo

Thank you for your
present. *sing. inform.*

Muchas gracias por su regalo.
moochahs grah-seeyahs por
soo reh-ghahlo

Thank you for your
present. *sing. form.*

Gracias por los regalos.
grah-seeyahs por los reh-ghahlos

Thanks for the presents.

**Muchas gracias por los
regalos.** moochahs grah-seeyahs
por los reh-ghahlos

Many thanks for the
presents.

**Gracias por todos estos
regalos.** grah-seeyahs por todos
ehstos reh-ghahlos

Thanks for all these
presents.

Gracias por pagar.
grah-seeyahs por pahghahr

Thanks for paying.

Gracias por poder estar aquí.
grah-seeyahs por podehr
ehstahr ahkee

Thanks for having me/us.

Language Tip

The English word "for" is generally translated into Spanish
as *para*: *Es para usted* (That's for you). An exception is
the expression "Thanks for...". The Spanish here uses
the preposition *por* : *Gracias por su regalo* (Thanks for your
present).

Culture Tip

When you're out with a group of people, it is very likely that you will be invited for a drink. Show your appreciation by ordering and paying for the next round.

Similarly, if you're eating out in Spain or Latin America, the custom is to split the bill evenly across the number of people in the group, so that everyone pays the same amount.

The adjective *bonito/a* can be applied to a wide range of things you will be shown or introduced to:

Es una ... muy bonita. ♀
ehs <u>oo</u>nah ... mwee bo<u>nee</u>tah

That is a very beautiful ...

ciudad
see<u>oo</u>-<u>dahd</u>

iglesia
ee<u>gleh</u>-seeyah

¡Qué bonito! ♂ keh bo<u>nee</u>to

How beautiful!

¡Qué regalo más bonito!
keh <u>reh</u>-ghahlo mahs bo<u>nee</u>to

What a beautiful present!

Language Tip

Qué (how) is often used in exlamations: *¡Qué bonito!* (How beautiful!). When used together with *más* (which translates as: "more") it means "what a": *¡Qué regalo más bonito!* (What a beautiful present!).

Es un regalo muy bonito.
ehs oon <u>reh</u>-ghahlo mwee bo<u>nee</u>to

That is a very beautiful present.

Es una habitación muy bonita.
ehs <u>oo</u>nah ahbeetah-<u>seeyon</u> mwee bo<u>nee</u>tah

This is a very nice room.

Son regalos muy buenos.
son <u>reh</u>-ghahlos mwee <u>bweh</u>nos

These are very good presents.

¿Dónde los puedo comprar? ♂
<u>don</u>deh los <u>pweh</u>do kom<u>prahr</u>

Where can I buy them?

¿Dónde las puedo comprar? ♀
<u>don</u>deh lahs <u>pweh</u>do kom<u>prahr</u>

Where can I buy them?

Language Tip

If a verb is preceded by an article <u>without</u> a noun, this article takes the place of the noun. For example, replace *Quiero la leche* (I want the milk) with *La quiero* (I want it), and instead of *¿Dónde puedo comprar los regalos?* (Where can I buy the presents?) simply ask *¿Dónde los puedo comprar?* (Where can I buy them?).

Son … muy buenas. ♀
son … mwee <u>bweh</u>nahs

These are very good …

gafas de sol
<u>ghah</u>fahs deh sol

aletas
ah-<u>leh</u>tahs

galletas
ghahl-<u>yeh</u>tahs

Communication Difficulties

In case you find it difficult to understand what is being said simply ask:

¿Perdón? pehr<u>don</u>   Excuse me?

¿Cómo? <u>ko</u>mo   What was that?

¿Qué? keh   What?

If you wish to consult this guide to look up an expression and want someone to wait for a moment, say:

Perdón, necesito un poco de   Excuse me, I need
tiempo. pehr<u>don</u> nehseh<u>see</u>to   a little more time.
oon <u>po</u>ko deh tee<u>yeh</u>mpo

Perdón, necesito ver esto.   Excuse me, I have to
pehr<u>don</u> nehseh<u>see</u>to behr <u>ehs</u>to   to look this up.

Perdón, necesito tiempo para   Excuse me, I need time
ver esto. pehr<u>don</u> nehseh<u>see</u>to   to look this up.
tee<u>yeh</u>mpo <u>pah</u>rah behr <u>ehs</u>to

Language Tip

Para (for) is also used before verbs such as *ver* (to see). In this case it means "in order to": *para ver* (in order to see).

Está aquí. eh<u>stah</u> ah<u>kee</u>   Here it is.

No está aquí. no eh<u>stah</u> ah<u>kee</u>   It's not here.

A typical reply would be:

Hay tiempo. eye tee<u>yeh</u>mpo   There is plenty of time.

Tengo tiempo. <u>teh</u>ngo tee<u>yeh</u>mpo   I have time.

You can also expand your vocabulary by learning new words. If you want to know the name of something point at it and ask:

¿Qué es? keh ehs   What is that?

¿Qué es esto? keh ehs <u>ehs</u>to   What is that (there)?

¿Cómo se llama?   What is this called?
<u>ko</u>mo seh <u>yah</u>mah

¿Cómo se llama esto?   What is this here called?
<u>ko</u>mo seh <u>yah</u>mah <u>ehs</u>to

If you are met with an air of surprise or bewilderment, you may have said something wrong or incomprehensible. Ask what you did wrong:

¿Qué está mal? keh ehs<u>tah</u> mahl   What's wrong?

¿Está mal? ehs<u>tah</u> mahl   Is that wrong?

Language Tip

Normally a question in Spanish opens with an interrogative as the example above did with *qué* (what). It is also possible to change the intonation of a statement and thereby turn it into a question. This way *Está mal.* (That is wrong.) can become *¿Está mal?* (Is that wrong?).

¿No está bien? no ehs<u>tah</u> bee<u>yeh</u>n   Is that wrong (not right)?

¿Algo no está bien?   Is something wrong
<u>ah</u>lgo no es<u>tah</u> bee<u>yeh</u>n   (not right)?

¿Qué no está bien?   What was wrong
keh no ehs<u>tah</u> bee<u>yeh</u>n   (not right)?

If you are not sure whether the word you used was correct, point at the object in question and ask:

¿ ... [repeat the word] no   Is ... that not right?
está bien? no ehs<u>tah</u> bee<u>yeh</u>n

¿No es un ... [♂ word]?   Is that not a ...?
no ehs oon

¿Esto no es un ... [♂ word]?   That is not a ...?
<u>ehs</u>to no ehs oon

¿Esto no es una ... [♀ word]?   That is not a ...?
<u>ehs</u>to no ehs <u>oo</u>nah

¿No se llama ... [word]?   Is that not called ...?
no seh <u>yah</u>mah

¿Esto no se llama ... [word]?   That is not called ...?
<u>ehs</u>to no seh <u>yah</u>mah

Small Talk

Health

It is common to ask about people's well-being, even if you do not expect a lengthy answer.

¿Cómo estás? <u>ko</u>mo eh<u>stahs</u>   How are you? *sing. inform.*

¿Cómo está? <u>ko</u>mo eh<u>stah</u>   How are you? *sing. form.*

Culture Tip

Spanish distinguishes between two forms of "you". The informal *tu* is used when speaking to children, family or close friends, the formal *usted* is used to show respect.
Use of the informal form varies by country: in Spain, people use informal address frequently, while in some Latin American countries the *usted* form is used more widely. To avoid offense, always use the *usted* form until the person you are speaking with switches to the informal, or invites you to use *tu*.

Inquiries about someone's well-being are usually answered positively:

Bien. bee<u>yehn</u>   Good/fine/well.

Muy bien. mwee bee<u>yehn</u>   Very well.

Muy bien, gracias.   Very well, thank you.
mwee bee<u>yehn</u> <u>grah</u>-seeyahs

Bien, gracias. bee<u>yehn</u>   Fine, thank you.
<u>grah</u>-seeyahs

Estoy bien, gracias.   I'm doing fine, thank you.
eh<u>stoyee</u> bee<u>yehn</u> <u>grah</u>-seeyahs

Estamos bien, gracias.
ehs*tah*mos bee*yehn* *grah*-seeyahs

We're doing fine, thank you.

No podría ir mejor.
no pod*ree*-ah eer meh*khor*

Things couldn't be better.

¿Y usted? ee oos*tehd*

And how are you? *sing. form.*

There are situations where the answer might be less positive:

No muy bien.
no mwee bee*yehn*

Not very well.

No demasiado bien.
no dehmah*seeyah*-doh bee*yehn*

Not too well.

Mal. mahl

Badly.

Muy mal. mwee mahl

Very badly.

Podría ir mejor.
pod*ree*-ah eer meh*khor*

Things could be better.

Podría ir mucho mejor.
pod*ree*-ah eer *moo*cho meh*khor*

Things could be much better.

If someone has been going through a hard time lately, you could ask:

¿Cómo estás hoy?
*ko*mo ehs*tahs* oye

How are you doing today? *sing. inform.*

¿Cómo está hoy?
komo ehs*tah* oyee

How are you doing today? *sing. form.*

¿Estás mejor?
ehs*tahs* meh*khor*

Do you feel better? *sing. inform.*

¿Ya está mejor?
yah ehs*tah* meh*khor*

Are you feeling better? *sing. form.*

¿Estás mejor hoy?
ehstahs mehkhor oyee

Are you feeling any
better today? *sing. inform.*

Hopefully the answer will be:

Mejor. mehkhor

Better.

Sí, estoy mejor.
see ehstoyee mehkhor

Yes, I am better.

Ya estamos mejor.
yah ehstahmos mehkhor

We're feeling better
already.

Hoy estoy mejor.
oyee ehstoyee mehkhor

I am feeling better today.

Estoy mucho mejor.
ehstoyee moocho mehkhor

I am much better.

Hoy ya estoy mucho mejor.
oyee yah ehstoyee moocho
mehkhor

I am much better today.

If there's no improvement, you can always try to cheer the person you're talking to up a little bit:

Con el tiempo va a ir mejor.
kon ehl teeyehmpo bah ah eer
mehkhor

Things will get better
with time.

Language Tip

In connection with *a* and another verb, *ir* can also be used to express the future: *Mañana va a ser mejor* means "Things will be better tomorrow".

Background

One of the first questions usually asked is where someone comes from. To ask or answer this, you could say:

¿De dónde eres?
deh <u>don</u>deh <u>e</u>hrehs

Where are you from?
sing. inform.

¿De dónde es usted?
deh <u>don</u>deh ehs oos<u>tehd</u>

Where are you from?
sing. form.

Soy de Estados Unidos.*
soyee deh ehs<u>tah</u>dos oo<u>nee</u>dos

I'm from the United States.

Somos de Estados Unidos.
<u>so</u>mos deh ehs<u>tah</u>dos oo<u>nee</u>dos

We're from the United States.

¿Y de dónde en Estados Unidos?
ee deh <u>don</u>deh ehn ehs<u>tah</u>dos oo<u>nee</u>dos

And from where in the United States?

Soy de... [place/city].
soyee deh

I'm from ...

Somos de... [place/city].
<u>so</u>mos deh

We're from ...

¿Dónde vives?
<u>don</u>deh <u>bee</u>behs

Where do you live?
sing. inform.

¿Dónde vive usted?
<u>don</u>deh <u>bee</u>beh oos<u>tehd</u>

Where do you live?
sing. form.

Vivo en ... [place/city]. <u>bee</u>bo ehn

I live in ...

Vivimos en ... [place/city].
bee<u>bee</u>mos ehn

We live in ...

---

* **Canadá** kahnah<u>dah</u>
   Gran Bretaña grahn breh<u>tah</u>nyah

Canada
Great Britain

¿No es cerca de ... [place/city]?   Isn't that near ...?
no ehs <u>sehr</u>kah deh

Sí, es cerca de ... [place/city].   Yes, it is near ...
see ehs <u>sehr</u>kah deh

Sí, es muy cerca   Yes, that is very close to ...
de ... [place/city].
see ehs mwee <u>sehr</u>kah deh

No, no es cerca de ... [place/city]. No, it is not near ...
no no ehs <u>sehr</u>kah deh

Vivo cerca de ... [place/city].   I live near ...
<u>bee</u>bo <u>sehr</u>kah deh

Vivimos cerca de ... [place/city]. We live near ...
bee<u>bee</u>mos <u>sehr</u>kah deh

Language Tip

Don't get confused by the repeated use of *no* in Spanish,
also known as the double negative. As it means both "no"
and "not", you will find it is sometimes repeated in sentences: *No, no es cerca de...* (<u>No</u>, that's <u>not</u> near ...).

¿Qué hay cerca   What's near ...?
de ... [place/city]?
keh eye <u>sehr</u>kah deh

... [place/city] está cerca   ... is near ...
de ... [place/city].
eh<u>stah</u> <u>sehr</u>kah deh

¿Eres de aquí? <u>eh</u>rehs deh ah<u>kee</u>   Are you from here?
sing. inform.

¿Usted es de aquí?   Are you from here?
oo<u>stehd</u> ehs deh ah<u>kee</u>   *sing. form.*

Sí, soy de aquí.
see soyee deh ah<u>kee</u>

Yes, I'm from here.

Sí, somos de aquí.
see <u>so</u>mos deh ah<u>kee</u>

Yes, we're from here.

No soy de aquí.
no soyee deh ah<u>kee</u>

I'm not from here.

No, no somos de aquí.
no no <u>so</u>mos deh ah<u>kee</u>

No, we're not from here.

Pero vivo cerca de aquí.
pehro <u>bee</u>bo <u>sehr</u>kah deh ah<u>kee</u>

But I live nearby.

Maybe the person you are talking to has visited your country:

Ya he estado en Estados Unidos*.
yah eh eh<u>stah</u>do ehn eh<u>stah</u>dos oo<u>nee</u>dos

I've been to the United States before.

Ya hemos estado en Estados Unidos.
yah <u>eh</u>mos eh<u>stah</u>do ehn eh<u>stah</u>dos oo<u>nee</u>dos

We've been to the United States before.

Language Tip

Use the auxiliary verb *he/hemos* and the participle *estado* (have been) to talk about something that you did in the past.

---

* **Canadá** kahnah<u>dah</u>   Canada
Gran Bretaña grahn breh<u>tah</u>nyah   Great Britain

You may also hear:

Estados Unidos* es muy bonita.
ehs<u>tah</u>dos oo<u>nee</u>dos ehs mwee bo<u>nee</u>to

The United States is very beautiful.

Estados Unidos me gusta.
ehs<u>tah</u>dos oo<u>nee</u>dos meh <u>goo</u>stah

I like the United States.

Estados Unidos nos gusta mucho.
ehs<u>tah</u>dos oo<u>nee</u>dos nos <u>goo</u>stah <u>moo</u>cho

We like the United States very much.

For even more detail, someone might say:

En Estados Unidos se puede comer pescado muy bien.
ehn ehs<u>tah</u>dos oo<u>nee</u>dos seh <u>pweh</u>deh ko<u>mehr</u> mwee bee<u>yehn</u>

One can eat very good fish in the United States.

En Estados Unidos hay mucho que ver.
ehn ehs<u>tah</u>dos oo<u>nee</u>dos eye <u>moo</u>cho keh behr

There is a lot to see in the United States.

Language Tip

Se means either "oneself" or "one" as in *Se come bien* (One can eat well).

---

* **Canadá** kahnah<u>dah</u>   Canada
  Gran Bretaña grahn breh<u>tah</u>nyah   Great Britain

You might wish to reply in return:

Sí, pero aquí también.
see pehro ah<u>kee</u> tahmbee<u>yehn</u>

Yes, but here as well.

Aquí también se come muy bien. ah<u>kee</u> tahmbee<u>yehn</u> seh <u>ko</u>meh mwee bee<u>yehn</u>

Here one can also eat very well.

Aquí también se puede ver mucho. ah<u>kee</u> tahmbee<u>yehn</u> seh <u>pweh</u>deh behr <u>moo</u>cho

There is a lot to see here as well.

It may be that the person you are speaking with has already been to your hometown:

Ya he estado en … [place/city].
yah eh ehs<u>tah</u>do ehn

I've already been to …

Ya hemos estado en … [place/city].
yah ehmos ehs<u>tah</u>do ehn

We've already been to …

… [place/city] me gusta mucho.
meh <u>goo</u>stah <u>moo</u>cho

I like ... very much.

… [place/city] nos gusta mucho.
nos <u>goo</u>stah <u>moo</u>cho

We like ... very much.

Age

The following sentences allow you to ask someone his or her age and to talk about how old you are.

¿Cuántos años tienes?
<u>kwahn</u>tos <u>ah</u>nyos tee<u>yeh</u>nehs
How old are you?
sing. inform.

¿Cuántos años tiene usted?
<u>kwahn</u>tos <u>ah</u>nyos tee<u>yeh</u>neh oo<u>steh</u>d
How old are you?
sing. form.

Tengo ... [age] años.
<u>teh</u>ngo ... <u>ah</u>nyos
I am ... years old.

Ya tengo ... [age] años.
yah <u>teh</u>ngo ... <u>ah</u>nyos
I am already ... years old.

Language Tip

The literal translation of the Spanish *tengo ... años* is "I have ... years". The numbers you'll need to tell someone your age are listed on page 109.

Yo también. yo tahm<u>beeyehn</u>
Me too.

Yo también tengo ... [age] años.
yo tahmbee<u>yehn</u> <u>teh</u>ngo ... <u>ah</u>nyos
I am also ... years old.

Yo tengo un año más.
yo <u>teh</u>ngo oon <u>ah</u>nyo mahs
I'm a year older.

Yo tengo dos años más.
yo <u>teh</u>ngo dos <u>ah</u>nyos mahs
I'm two years older.

Mañana voy a tener ...
[age] años. mah<u>nyah</u>nah
boyee ah teh<u>nehr</u>
I'll be ... tomorrow.

Language Tip

Más means *more* and can be used with a verb to refer to
any object: *Quiero más* (I want more).

Be tactful when asking someone his or her age in Spanish. Some
people would rather not tell you, in which case you may hear:

Muchos. <u>moo</u>chos   Many (years).

Demasiados. dehmah<u>seeyah</u>-dos   Too many.

Do You Like It?

You may want to tell others how much you enjoy something or a
particular place, or you want to ask others for their impressions.
You could say:

¿Te gusta?   Do you like it?
teh <u>goo</u>stah   *sing. inform.*

¿Le gusta?   Do you like it?
leh <u>goo</u>stah   *sing. form.*

You could reply:

Sí, me gusta. see meh <u>goo</u>stah   Yes, I like it.

Sí, me gusta mucho.   Yes, I like it very much.
see meh <u>goo</u>stah <u>moo</u>cho

Sí, nos gusta mucho.
see nos goostah moocho

Yes, we like it very much.

Sí, me gusta todo.
see meh goostah todo

Yes, I'm enjoying
everything.

Sí, aquí nos gusta todo.
see ahkee nos goostah todo

Yes, we are enjoying
everything here.

Sí, me gusta más que …
[name of the place/resort].
see meh goostah mahs keh

Yes, I like it better
than …

Language Tip

To compare things, use *más que* (more than): *Come más*
que… (He eats more than …); *Me gusta más que…* (I like it
better than …).
In such comparisons the Spanish *que* means "than".
Más (more) is used for comparative clauses with adjectives:
bonito (nice/beautiful) – *más bonito* (nicer/more beautiful) –
el más bonito (the nicest/most beautiful).

Or perhaps you prefer something else:

¿No te gusta?
no teh goostah

Don't you like it?
sing. inform.

¿No le gusta?
no leh goostah

Don't you like it?
sing. form.

No, no me gusta.
no no meh goostah

No, I don't like it.

No me gusta nada.
no meh <u>goo</u>stah <u>nah</u>dah

I don't like it at all.

No, no nos gusta nada.
no no nos <u>goo</u>stah <u>nah</u>dah

No we don't like it at all.

No es nada bonito.
no ehs <u>nah</u>dah bo<u>nee</u>to

This isn't nice at all.

Language Tip

If you want to put special emphasis on negation, you can combine *no* (not) and *nada* (nothing) as in the example above. This translates into "not at all".

… [place/city] me gusta menos que … [place/city].
meh <u>goo</u>stah <u>meh</u>nos keh

I like … less than …

Language Tip

Use *menos que* (less than) to compare things as well: *Me gusta menos que el otro* (I like it less than the other one) or *Es menos bonito que el otro* (It is less beautiful than the other one).

If you are having a particularly good time and would like to express how much you would enjoy living in a place permanently you could say:

Aquí se vive muy bien.　　Life's very good here.
ahkee seh beebeh mwee beeyehn

Me gustaría vivir aquí.　　I'd like to live here.
meh goostahree-ah beebeer ahkee

On the other hand you might not feel quite that strongly:

No me gustaría vivir aquí　　I would not want to
todo el tiempo.　　live here permanently.
no meh goostahree-ah beebeer
ahkee todo ehl teeyehmpo

Talking About Vacation Activities

To talk about what you want to do during your trip, try these phrases:

Aquí hay mucho que hacer.　　There are plenty of things
ahkee eye moocho keh ahsehr　　to do here.

Aquí se puede hacer mucho.　　There are plenty of things
ahkee seh pwehdeh ahsehr moocho　　one can do.

Hago muchas cosas.　　There is plenty for me
ahgo moochahs kosahs　　to do.

Hacemos muchas cosas.　　There is plenty for us
ahsehmos moochahs kosahs　　to do.

Hay mucho que ver.　　There's a lot to see.
eye moocho keh behr

Nos gusta ver muchas cosas.
nos <u>goo</u>stah behr <u>moo</u>chahs <u>ko</u>sahs

We enjoy visiting/seeing many things.

Vemos muchas cosas.
<u>beh</u>mos <u>moo</u>chahs <u>ko</u>sahs

We visit/see a lot of things.

Todos los días veo muchas cosas.
<u>to</u>dos los <u>dee</u>ahs beho <u>moo</u>chahs <u>ko</u>sahs

I visit many sights every day.

Pero no se puede ver todo.
pehro no seh <u>pweh</u>deh behr <u>to</u>do

But you can't visit/see everything.

Vamos muy tarde a la cama.
<u>bah</u>mos mwee <u>tahr</u>de ah lah <u>kah</u>mah

We go to bed very late.

Todos los días voy a la …
<u>to</u>dos los <u>dee</u>ahs boyee ah lah

Every day I go to the …

piscina
pees-<u>see</u>nah

playa
<u>plah</u>yah

ciudad
<u>seew</u>dahd

Todas las noches nos vamos a beber algo. <u>to</u>dahs lahs <u>no</u>chehs nos <u>bah</u>mos ah beh<u>behr</u> <u>ahl</u>go

We go out for a drink every night.

If you want to rest during your vacation you could say:

No hago nada. no <u>ah</u>go <u>nah</u>dah

I'm not doing anything.

Nos gusta no hacer nada.
nos <u>goo</u>stah no ah<u>sehr</u> <u>nah</u>dah

We like to do nothing.

Me gusta dormir mucho.
meh goostah dormeer moocho

I like to sleep a lot.

Es lo que más me gusta.
ehs lo keh mahs meh goostah

That's what I like best.

But sometimes you may not have many choices:

Aquí no se puede hacer nada.
ahkee no seh pwehdeh ahsehr
nahdah

There is nothing
to do here.

No hay nada para ver.
no eye nahdah pahrah behr

There is nothing to see.

Someone might ask you how long you are staying:

¿Cuántos días estás aquí?
kwahntos deeahs ehstahs ahkee

For how many days are
you here? *sing. inform.*

¿Cuántos días lleva aquí?
kwahntos deeahs yehbah ahkee

How many days have you
been here so far? *sing. form.*

¿Cuántos días vas a estar aquí?
kwahntos deeahs bahs ah ehstahr
ahkee

How many days are you
going to be here? *sing.*
inform.

¿Cuántos días va a estar aquí?
kwahntos deeahs bah ah ehstahr
ahkee

How many days are
you going to be here?
sing. form.

Voy a estar aquí un día.
boyee ah ehstahr ahkee oon deeah

I am staying here for
one day.

Vamos a estar aquí dos días.
bahmos ah ehstahr ahkee dos deeahs

We are staying here for
two days.

Ya estoy aquí hace dos días.
yah ehstoyee ahkee ahseh dos deeahs

I have been here for two
days already.

Vamos a estar aquí dos días más. bahmos ah ehstahr ahkee dos deeahs mahs

We will be here for another two days.

Nos vamos a ir mañana. nos bahmos ah eer mahnyahnah

We will leave tomorrow.

Language Tip

If you add *me, te, se* or *nos* before the Spanish verb *ir* (to go), it can be used to mean "to depart" or "to leave" as in: *Me voy* (I'm leaving).

Weather

The weather is a popular and easy conversation topic:

Hace buen tiempo. ahseh bwehn teeyehmpo

The weather is nice.

Hace muy buen tiempo. ahseh mwee bwehn teeyehmpo

The weather is very nice.

Aquí hace buen tiempo. ahkee ahseh bwehn teeyehmpo

The weather is nice here.

Hace muy buen tiempo aquí. ahseh mwee bwehn teeyehmpo ahkee

The weather is very nice here.

Hoy hace muy buen tiempo. oyee ahseh mwee bwehn teeyehmpo

The weather is very nice today.

El tiempo aquí es muy bueno. ehl teeyehmpo ahkee ehs mwee bwehno

The weather here is very nice.

El tiempo aquí es bueno todos los días. ehl <u>tee</u>yehmpo ah<u>kee</u> ehs <u>bweh</u>no <u>to</u>dos los <u>dee</u>ahs

Here the weather is always nice.

Language Tip

As you see in the examples above, the Spanish verb *hacer* (to do/to make) is used when describing the weather: *Hace …* It (the weather) is …

Unfortunately, there is no guarantee against bad weather:

Hace mal tiempo.
<u>ah</u>seh mahl <u>tee</u>yehmpo

The weather is bad.

Hace muy mal tiempo.
<u>ah</u>seh mwee mahl <u>tee</u>yehmpo

The weather is very bad.

Hoy el tiempo no es muy bueno. oyee ehl <u>tee</u>yehmpo no ehs mwee <u>bweh</u>no

The weather today is not very nice.

No, pero mañana va a ser mejor. no pehro mah<u>nyah</u>nah bah ah sehr meh<u>khor</u>

No, but tomorrow it will be better.

No, pero no se puede hacer nada. no pehro no seh <u>pweh</u>deh ah<u>sehr</u> <u>nah</u>dah

No, but there is nothing you can do about it.

Podría hacer mejor tiempo.
po<u>dree</u>-ah ah<u>sehr</u> meh<u>khor</u> <u>tee</u>yehmpo

The weather could be better.

El tiempo aquí no es muy bueno. ehl <u>tee</u>yehmpo ah<u>kee</u> no ehs mwee <u>bweh</u>no

The weather isn't particularly nice here.

No, pero me gusta. No, but I like it.
no pehro meh <u>goo</u>stah

More likely, though, it will be too hot rather than too cold.

¡Qué calor! keh kah<u>lor</u> What heat!

¡Qué calor hace! keh kah<u>lor</u> <u>ah</u>seh It's so hot!

¡Hace mucho calor! It is very hot!
<u>ah</u>seh <u>moo</u>cho kah<u>lor</u>

¡Hace demasiado calor! It is too hot!
<u>ah</u>seh dehmah<u>seey</u>ah-doh kah<u>lor</u>

¡Tengo mucho calor! I'm very hot!
<u>teh</u>ngo <u>moo</u>cho kah<u>lor</u>

¡Tenemos demasiado calor! It is too hot for us!
teh<u>neh</u>mos dehmah<u>seey</u>ah-doh
kah<u>lor</u>

¡Hoy tengo demasiado calor! It is too hot for me today!
oyee <u>teh</u>ngo dehmah<u>seey</u>ah-doh
kah<u>lor</u>

Esta tarde va a hacer menos It will not be so hot
calor. <u>eh</u>stah <u>tah</u>rdeh bah ah anymore this afternoon/
ah<u>seh</u>r <u>meh</u>nos kah<u>lor</u> this evening.

You could also compare the weather where you are to the weather back home:

Hace más calor que It is hotter than in …
en … [place/city].
<u>ah</u>seh mahs kah<u>lor</u> keh ehn

Aquí hace menos calor que en … [place/city].
ah<u>kee</u> <u>ah</u>seh <u>meh</u>nos kah<u>lor</u> keh ehn

It is colder here than in …

El tiempo aquí es mejor que en … [place/city].
ehl <u>teeye</u>hmpo ah<u>kee</u> ehs meh<u>khor</u> keh ehn

The weather here is better than in …

Paying Compliments

Small compliments can work wonders. You might want to say something nice to your new friends, for example about what they are wearing:

Tu … es muy bonito. ♂
too … ehs mwee bo<u>nee</u>to

Your … is very nice.
sing. inform.

vestido
behs<u>tee</u>do

sombrero
som<u>breh</u>ro

anillo
ah<u>neel</u>-yo

Su … es muy bonita. ♀
soo … ehs mwee bo<u>nee</u>tah

Your … is very nice.
sing. form.

blusa
<u>bloo</u>sah

corbata
kor<u>bah</u>tah

Esto te va muy bien.*
ehsto teh bah mwee beeyehn

This suits you very
well. *sing. inform.*

Esto le va muy bien.
ehsto leh bah mwee beeyehn

This suits you very
well. *sing. form.*

Esto es muy bonito. ♂
ehsto ehs mwee boneeto

That is very beautiful.

Esto también me gustaría.
ehsto tahmbeeyehn meh
goostahree-ah

I would like that
very much as well.

You may also wish to show someone your affection:

¡Eres el mejor! ♂
ehrehs ehl mehkhor

You're the best!
sing. inform.

¡Eres la mejor! ♀
ehrehs lah mehkhor

You're the best!
sing. inform.

---

* Idiomatic expression:
Te/Le va bien. teh/leh bah beeyehn It suits you very well.

Accommodations

Finding a Room

If you are looking for an available room, ask:

¿Tiene una habitación?　　　Do you have a room?
teeyehneh oonah ahbeetah-seeyon

¿Tiene habitaciones?　　　Do you have any rooms?
teeyehneh ahbeetah-seeyonehs

Necesito una habitación.　　I need a room.
nehsehseeto oonah ahbeetah-seeyon

Necesitamos dos habitaciones.　We need two rooms.
nehsehseetahmos dos
ahbeetah-seeyonehs

To be more precise in your search say:

¿Tiene una habitación con　　Do you have a room
una cama? teeyehneh oonah　with one bed?
ahbeetah-seeyon kon oonah kahmah

¿Tiene una habitación con　　Do you have a room
dos camas? teeyehneh oonah　with two beds?
ahbeetah-seeyon kon dos kahmahs

Necesito una habitación con　I need a room
una cama. nehsehseeto oonah　with one bed.
ahbeetah-seeyon kon oonah kahmah

Necesitamos una habitación　We need a room
con dos camas.　　　　　　with two beds.
nehsehseeto oonah ahbeetah-seeyon
kon dos kahmahs

Necesitamos dos habitaciones con dos camas. nehsehsee-<u>tah</u>mos dos ahbeetah-<u>seeyon</u>ehs kon dos <u>kah</u>mahs

We need two rooms with two beds.

Necesitamos una habitación con una cama y otra habitación con dos camas. nehsehsee-<u>tah</u>mos <u>oo</u>nah ahbeetah-<u>seeyon</u> kon <u>oo</u>nah <u>kah</u>mah y <u>o</u>trah ahbeetah-<u>seeyon</u> kon dos <u>kah</u>mahs

We need one room with one bed and another room with two beds.

And when asked when and for how long you want the room:

¿Para cuándo? <u>pah</u>rah <u>kwahn</u>do
For when?

¿Hasta cuándo? <u>ahs</u>tah <u>kwahn</u>do
Until when?

¿De cuándo hasta cuándo? deh <u>kwahn</u>do <u>ahs</u>tah <u>kwahn</u>do
From when until when?

¿Hasta qué día? <u>ahs</u>tah keh <u>dee</u>ah
Until which day?

¿De qué día hasta qué día? deh keh <u>dee</u>ah <u>ahs</u>tah keh <u>dee</u>ah
From which day until which day?

¿Para cuántas noches? <u>pah</u>rah <u>kwahn</u>tahs <u>no</u>chehs
For how many nights?

You could reply:

Es para hoy y mañana. ehs <u>pah</u>rah oyee ee mah<u>nyah</u>nah
It's for today and tomorrow.

De hoy hasta mañana. deh oyee <u>ahs</u>tah mah<u>nyah</u>nah
From today until tomorrow.

Es para una noche.
ehs <u>pah</u>rah <u>oo</u>nah <u>no</u>cheh

It's for one night.

Es para dos noches.
ehs <u>pah</u>rah dos <u>no</u>chehs

It's for two nights

Hasta el día uno.
<u>ah</u>stah ehl <u>dee</u>ah <u>oo</u>no

Until the first.

Hasta el día …
<u>ah</u>stah ehl <u>dee</u>ah

Until the …

See page 109 for numbers.

De hoy hasta el día dos.
deh oyee <u>ah</u>stah ehl <u>dee</u>ah dos

From today until
the second.

Hasta el … <u>ah</u>stah ehl

Until …

See page 111 for days of the week.

If there's no vacancy you could ask:

¿Y dónde hay algo?
ee <u>don</u>deh eye <u>ah</u>lgo

And where can I
find something?

**¿Dónde hay habitaciones
cerca de aquí?** <u>don</u>deh eye
ahbeetah-<u>seeyo</u>nehs <u>sehr</u>kah
deh ah<u>kee</u>

Where can I get a room
around here?

Furnishings and Extras

You may want to specify a few more requirements for the room:

Me gustaría una habitación con ... meh goostah-<u>ree</u>ah <u>oo</u>nah ahbeetah-<u>seeyon</u> kon

I'd like to have a room with ...

lavabo
lah<u>bah</u>bo

bañera
bah<u>nyeh</u>rah

ducha
<u>doo</u>chah

wáter
<u>bah</u>tehr

Culture Tip

In Spain, bathrooms often have two faucets, one for hot water and one for cold water. Be careful with the hot water: it can be boiling hot!

¿Hay ... en la habitación?
eye ... ehn lah ahbeetah-<u>seeyon</u>

Does the room have a ...?

televisor
tehlehbee-<u>sor</u>

teléfono
teh<u>leh</u>fono

nevera neh<u>beh</u>rah
LA: frigorífico
LA: freego-<u>ree</u>feeko

ventilador
behnteelah-<u>dor</u>

¿Es con …? ehs kon   Does it include …?

desayuno
dehsahl-<u>yoo</u>no

comida ko<u>mee</u>dah
LA: almuerzo
LA: ahl<u>mwehr</u>-so

cena
<u>seh</u>nah

**Por favor, quiero la habitación
más bonita.** por fahbor kee<u>yeh</u>ro
lah ahbeetah-<u>seeyon</u> mahs bo<u>nee</u>tah

I would like the nicest
room, please.

**Nos gustaría tener la
habitación más grande.**
nos goostah-<u>ree</u>ah teh<u>nehr</u> lah
ahbeetah-<u>seeyon</u> mahs <u>grahn</u>deh

We would like the
largest room.

Prices

If you want to know how much the rooms are, ask:

¿Cuánto cuesta una noche?
<u>kwahn</u>to <u>kwehs</u>tah <u>oo</u>nah <u>no</u>cheh

How much is it for
one night?

¿Cuánto cuestan dos noches?
<u>kwahn</u>to <u>kwehs</u>tahn dos <u>no</u>chehs

How much is it for
two nights?

¿Cuánto cuesta por noche?
<u>kwahn</u>to <u>kwehs</u>tah por <u>no</u>cheh

How much is it per night?

**¿Cuánto cuesta por todo el
tiempo?** <u>kwahn</u>to <u>kwehs</u>tah
por todo ehl <u>teeyehm</u>po

How much is it for
the whole time?

¿Cuánto cuesta con …?
kwahnto kwehstah kon

How much is it with …?

desayuno
dehsahl-yoono

comida komeedah
LA: almuerzo
LA: ahlmwehr-so

cena
sehnah

¿Cuándo hay que pagar?
kwahndo eye keh pahgahr

When do I have to pay?

¿Tengo que pagar hoy?
tehngo keh pahgahr oyee

Do I have to pay today?

¿Puedo pagar mañana?
pwehdo pahgahr mahnyahnah

Can I pay tomorrow?

Language Tip

Tener by itself means "to have". When used with *que* it means "must", as in *Tengo que comer algo* (I must eat something).
Hay que means "one must/has to".

But perhaps the room is too expensive for you:

La habitación cuesta mucho.
lah ahbeetah-<u>seeyon</u> <u>kweh</u>stah
<u>moo</u>cho

The room is expensive.

**La habitación cuesta
demasiado.** lah ahbeetah-<u>seeyon</u>
<u>kweh</u>stah dehmah<u>seeyah</u>-do

The room is too expensive.

**Estas habitaciones cuestan
demasiado.**
<u>eh</u>stahs ahbeetah-<u>seeyon</u>ehs
<u>kweh</u>stahn dehmah<u>seeyah</u>-do

These rooms cost too
much.

**¿Cuesta menos por más
noches?** <u>kweh</u>stah <u>meh</u>nos
por mahs <u>no</u>chehs

Would more nights cost
less?

Quiero pagar menos.
kee<u>yeh</u>ro pah<u>gahr</u> <u>meh</u>nos

I want to pay less.

You might want to have a look at the room before you decide:

Me gustaría ver la habitación.
meh goostah-<u>ree</u>ah behr lah
ahbeetah-<u>seeyon</u>

I would like to see
the room.

**Nos gustaría ver las
habitaciones.** nos goostah-<u>ree</u>ah
behr lahs ahbeetah-<u>seeyon</u>ehs

We would like to see
the rooms.

**Por favor, quiero ver la
habitación.** por fah<u>bor</u>
kee<u>yeh</u>ro behr lah ahbeetah-<u>seeyon</u>

I want to see the
room, please.

Making a Decision

If you decide to take the room, you can say:

La habitación me gusta.   I like the room.
lah ahbeetah-<u>see</u>yon meh <u>goo</u>stah

Esta habitación me gusta.   I like this room.
<u>eh</u>stah ahbeetah-<u>see</u>yon meh <u>goo</u>stah

La habitación es bonita.   The room is nice.
lah ahbeetah-<u>see</u>yon ehs bo<u>nee</u>tah

Esta habitación es muy bonita.   This room is very nice.
<u>eh</u>stah ahbeetah-<u>see</u>yon ehs mwee
bo<u>nee</u>tah

La habitación está bien.   The room is fine.
lah ahbeetah-<u>see</u>yon eh<u>stah</u> bee<u>yehn</u>

La cama es muy buena.   The bed is very good.
lah <u>kah</u>mah ehs mwee <u>bweh</u>nah

Language Tip

Está bien is an expression that means "That's OK". The verb
estar is always used in this expression regardless of whether
it describes a permanent or a temporary state.

If you don't want to take the room, say so:

No quiero esta habitación.   I don't want this room.
no kee<u>yeh</u>ro <u>eh</u>stah ahbeetah-<u>see</u>yon

No queremos dormir aquí.   We do not want to sleep
no keh<u>reh</u>mos dor<u>meer</u> ah<u>kee</u>   here.

No puedo dormir aquí.
no pwehdo dormeer ahkee

I cannot sleep here.

No voy a dormir aquí.
no boyee ah dormeer ahkee

I will not sleep here.

No vamos a dormir en esta habitación. no bahmos ah dormeer ehn ehstah ahbeetah-seeyon

We cannot sleep in this room.

You may want to give a reason for your decision:

La habitación no es bonita.
lah ahbeetah-seeyon no ehs boneetah

The room isn't nice.

Esta habitación no es muy bonita. ehstah ahbeetah-seeyon no ehs mwee boneetah

This room isn't very nice.

Esta habitación no es nada bonita. ehstah ahbeetah-seeyon no ehs nahdah boneetah

This room is not nice at all.

Esta habitación no me gusta.
ehstah ahbeetah-seeyon no meh goostah

I don't like this room.

La habitación no es muy grande. lah ahbeetah-seeyon no ehs mwee grahndeh

The room is not very large.

Hace mucho calor en esta habitación. ahseh moocho kahlor ehn ehstah ahbeetah-seeyon

It is very hot in this room.

Hace demasiado calor en esta habitación. ahseh dehmahseeyah-doh kahlor ehn ehstah ahbeetah-seeyon

It is too hot in this room.

No hace mucho calor en esta habitación. no ahseh moocho kahlor ehn ehstah ahbeetah-seeyon

It is not very warm in this room.

If you want to continue searching for a room you could ask:

¿Tiene otra habitación? teeyeh-neh otrah ahbeetah-seeyon

Do you have another room?

¿Tiene una habitación más bonita? teeyeh-neh oonah ahbeetah-seeyon mahs boneetah

Do you have a nicer room?

¿Tiene una habitación más grande? teeyeh-neh oonah ahbeetah-seeyon mahs grahndeh

Do you have a larger room?

¿Hay una habitación más bonita? eye oonah ahbeetah-seeyon mahs boneetah

Is there a nicer room?

Quiero otra habitación. keeyehro otrah ahbeetah-seeyon

I would like a different room.

Quiero una habitación más grande. keeyehro oonah ahbeetah-seeyon mahs grahndeh

I would like a larger room.

Quiero otra cama. keeyehro otrah kahmah

I want a different bed.

Necesitamos una habitación con una cama más. nehsehsee-tahmos oonah ahbeetah-seeyon kon oonah kahmah mahs

We need a room with one extra bed.

Quiero una habitación con una cama más grande.
keeyehro oonah ahbeetah-seeyon kon oonah kahmah mahs grahndeh

I want a room with a larger bed.

Por favor, quiero una habitación con una cama mejor. por fahbor keeyehro oonah ahbeetah-seeyon kon oonah kahmah mehkhor

I would like a room with a better bed, please.

Perhaps you prefer the room you see next:

Esta habitación me gusta más.
ehstah ahbeetah-seeyon meh goostah mahs

I like this room better.

Esta habitación me gusta más que la otra.
ehstah ahbeetah-seeyon meh goostah mahs keh lah otrah

I like this room better than the other one.

Esta habitación me gusta mucho más que la otra.
ehstah ahbeetah-seeyon meh goostah moocho mahs keh la otrah

I like this room much better than the other one.

Esta habitación es más bonita. ehstah ahbeetah-seeyon ehs mahs boneetah

This room is nicer.

Esta habitación es mucho más bonita. ehstah ahbeetah-seeyon ehs moocho mahs boneetah

This room is much nicer.

Esta habitación es más bonita que la otra.
ehstah ahbeetah-seeyon ehs mahs boneetah keh lah otrah

This room is nicer than the other one.

Esta habitación es más grande que la otra. ehstah ahbeetah-<u>see</u>yon ehs mahs <u>grahn</u>deh keh lah <u>o</u>trah

This room is larger than the other one.

Sí, aquí hace más calor. see ah<u>kee</u> <u>ah</u>seh mahs kah<u>lor</u>

Yes, it is warmer here.

Muy bien, aquí hace menos calor. mwee bee<u>yehn</u>, ah<u>kee</u> <u>ah</u>seh <u>meh</u>nos kah<u>lor</u>

Very good, it is cooler here.

Quiero esta habitación. kee<u>yeh</u>ro <u>eh</u>stah ahbeetah-<u>see</u>yon

I want this room.

Making Arrangements

Before you move into your room, you might want to clarify:

¿Qué habitación es? eh ahbeetah-<u>see</u>yon ehs

Which room is it?

Es la dos. ehs lah dos

It is room (number) two.

¿Ya podemos entrar en la habitación? yah po<u>deh</u>mos ehn<u>trahr</u> ehn lah ahbeetah-<u>see</u>yon

Can we go in the room yet?

¿Hasta cuándo se puede entrar aquí por la noche? <u>ah</u>stah <u>kwahn</u>do seh <u>pweh</u>deh ehn<u>trahr</u> ah<u>kee</u> por lah <u>no</u>cheh

Until when are you open at night?

Se puede entrar hasta las dos. seh <u>pweh</u>deh ehn<u>trahr</u> <u>ah</u>stah lahs dos

We are open until two o'clock.

Toda la noche. <u>to</u>dah lah <u>no</u>cheh

All through the night.

Now you want to find your way around:

¿Dónde está la habitación?
<u>don</u>deh ehs<u>tah</u> lah ahbeetah-<u>seeyon</u>

Where is the room?

Es por aquí. ehs por ah<u>kee</u>

This way.

Quiero ir a mi habitación.
kee<u>yeh</u>ro eer ah mee
ahbeetah-<u>seeyon</u>

I would like to go to
my room.

¿Dónde está? <u>don</u>deh ehs<u>tah</u>

Where is it?

¿Dónde está …? <u>don</u>deh ehs<u>tah</u>

Where is …?

la piscina
lah pees-<u>see</u>nah

el bar
ehl bahr

el restaurante
ehl rehstaw<u>rahn</u>-teh

el ascensor
ehl ahs-sehn<u>sor</u>
LA: el elevador
LA: ehl ehlebah-<u>dor</u>

Language Tip

As you have learned already, the verb *estar* is used to describe temporary situations. It is also used in questions about places and locations, even if it refers to a permanent, non-transitory, facility:
¿Dónde está mi habitación? Where is my room?

**¿Dónde se come por la
mañana?** <u>don</u>deh seh
<u>ko</u>meh por lah mah<u>nyah</u>nah

Where do you serve
breakfast?

¿Cuándo se come por la mañana? kwahndo seh komeh por lah mahnyahnah

When do you serve breakfast?

A las … [time]. ah lahs

At … o'clock.

De las … [time] hasta las … [time]. deh lahs … ahstah lahs

from … until … o'clock.

See page 109 for numbers.

¿Dónde se come aquí por la tarde? dondeh seh komeh ahkee por lah tahrdeh

Where is lunch/dinner served?

¿Cuándo se come aquí por la tarde? kwahndo seh komeh ahkee por lah tahrdeh

When is lunch/dinner served?

If you are already hungry and thirsty when you arrive, you may want to ask:

¿Dónde puedo comer algo? dondeh pwehdo komehr ahlgo

Where can I eat something?

¿Dónde podemos beber algo? dondeh podehmos behbehr ahlgo

Where can we get something to drink?

¿Dónde puedo comprar algo para comer? dondeh podehmos komprahr ahlgo pahrah komehr

Where can I buy some food?

¿Dónde podemos comprar algo para beber? dondeh podehmos komprahr ahlgo pahrah behbehr

Where can we buy something to drink?

¿Hay algo para beber en la habitación? eye <u>ahl</u>go <u>pah</u>rah beh<u>behr</u> ehn lah ahbeetah-<u>seeyon</u>

Is there anything to drink in the room?

Complaints

Things can go wrong even in the best of hotels. In this case you might want to inform the front desk:

Esto está roto. <u>eh</u>sto ehs<u>tah</u> <u>ro</u>to

This is broken.

El ... está roto. ♂
ehl ... ehs<u>tah</u> <u>ro</u>to

The ... is broken.

televisor
tehlehbee<u>sor</u>

ascensor
ahs-sehn<u>sor</u>
LA: elevador
LA: ehl ehlehbah-<u>dor</u>

Mi cama está rota.
mee <u>kah</u>mah ehs<u>tah</u> <u>ro</u>tah

My bed is broken.

La ... está rota. ♀
lah ... ehs<u>tah</u> <u>ro</u>tah

The ... is broken.

bañera
bah<u>nyeh</u>rah

ducha
<u>doo</u>chah

lámpara
<u>lahm</u>pahrah

If nothing is done about your complaint, speak up:

¡Hay que hacer algo!
aye keh ah<u>sehr</u> <u>ahl</u>go

Something has to be done!

¡Tiene que hacer algo!
tee<u>yeh</u>neh keh ahsehr ahlgo

You have to do something!

¿Qué se puede hacer?
keh seh <u>pweh</u>deh ah<u>sehr</u>

What can you do?

¿Qué va a hacer?
keh bah ah ah<u>sehr</u>

What will you do?

¿Cuándo va a hacer algo?
<u>kwahn</u>do seh bah ah ah<u>sehr</u> <u>ahl</u>go

When will you do something (about it)?

Departure

At some point you will have to inform the hotel when you plan to leave:

¿Qué día se va a ir?
keh <u>dee</u>ah seh bah ah eer

Which day are you planning to leave?

Me voy hoy. meh boyee oyee

I'm leaving today.

Nos vamos mañana.
nos <u>bah</u>mos mah<u>nyah</u>nah

We leave tomorrow.

Nos vamos a ir mañana.
nos <u>bah</u>mos ah eer mah<u>nyah</u>nah

We will leave tomorrow.

Me voy a ir mañana.
meh boyee ah eer mah<u>nyah</u>nah

I will leave tomorrow.

Nos vamos a ir mañana por la mañana. nos <u>bah</u>mos ah eer mah<u>nyah</u>nah por lah mah<u>nyah</u>nah

We will leave tomorrow morning.

Nos vamos el ... [date]. nos <u>bah</u>mos ehl

We leave on ...

Nos vamos a ir el ... [date]. nos <u>bah</u>mos ah eer ehl

We will leave on ...

See page 111 for days of the week.

¿Cuándo nos tenemos que ir? <u>kwahn</u>do nos teh<u>neh</u>mos keh eer

When do we have to leave?

¿Cuándo me tengo que ir de la habitación? <u>kwahn</u>do meh <u>teh</u>ngo keh eer deh lah ahbeetah-<u>seeyon</u>

When do I have to vacate the room?

El ... [date]. ehl

On ...

You might want to say good-bye with a compliment:

Se está muy bien aquí. seh ehs<u>tah</u> mwee bee<u>yehn</u> ah<u>kee</u>

One feels really comfortable here.

Puedo dormir muy bien aquí. <u>pweh</u>do dor<u>meer</u> mwee bee<u>yehn</u> ah<u>kee</u>

I can sleep very well here.

Aquí se puede dormir muy bien. ahkee seh pwehdeh dormeer mwee beeyehn

One sleeps very well here.

Todos los años nos gusta mucho. todos los ahnyos nos goostah moocho

We enjoy it every year.

Maybe you enjoyed your stay so much that you want to return:

¡Hasta otro año! ahstah otro ahnyo

Until the next time!

Vacation Activities

At the Restaurant

One of the first things you want to do is ask for a place to eat and find out what's on the menu there:

¿Se puede comer aquí?
seh pwehdeh komehr ahkee

Can one eat here?

¿Podemos comer aquí?
podehmos komehr ahkee

Can we eat here?

¿Es demasiado tarde para comer aquí? ehs
dehmahseeyah-do tahrdeh
pahrah komehr ahkee

Is it too late to eat here?

¿Qué hay para comer?
keh eye pahrah komehr

What do you have to eat?

¿Qué hay para beber?
keh eye pahrah behbehr

What do you have
to drink?

¿Puedo ver lo que hay?
pwehdo behr lo keh eye

Can I see what you have?

Culture Tip

Mealtimes in Spain and Latin America are generally later in the day. A small breakfast is between 7 and 10 am. Lunch is normally eaten at around 1 or 2 pm, and is the largest meal of the day. Dinner is around 8 or 9 pm, and diners sometimes linger until 11 pm or later.

Once you've decided what to eat, call the waiter or waitress:

Perdón! pehr<u>don</u>   Excuse me!

¡Por favor! por fah<u>bor</u>   Excuse me, please!

Por favor, quiero comer ...   I would like ..., please.
por fah<u>bor</u> kee<u>yeh</u>-ro ko<u>mehr</u>

una sopa
<u>oo</u>nah <u>so</u>pah

una ensalada
<u>oo</u>nah ehnsah<u>lah</u>-dah

un helado
oon eh<u>lah</u>do

Por favor, quiero beber ...   I'd like to drink ...,
por fah<u>bor</u> kee<u>yeh</u>-ro beh<u>behr</u>   please.

un café
oon kah<u>feh</u>

un agua mineral
oon <u>ah</u>gwah meeneh<u>rahl</u>

una cerveza
<u>oo</u>nah sehr<u>beh</u>sah

If the menu is illustrated with images or if you know what the
words mean, you could simply point at the name of the dish and
say:

Por favor, quiero esto.   I want this, please.
por fah<u>bor</u> kee<u>yeh</u>-ro <u>eh</u>sto

Me gustaría comer esto. I would like to eat this.
meh goostah<u>ree</u>-ah ko<u>mehr</u> <u>eh</u>sto

You could also ask to see what food they have:

¿Por favor, podría ver lo que Could I please see
hay para comer? por fah<u>bor</u> what you have?
pod<u>ree</u>ah behr lo keh eye <u>pah</u>rah
ko<u>mehr</u>

Me gustaría comer de esto. I'd like to eat this.
meh goostah<u>ree</u>-ah ko<u>mehr</u>
deh <u>eh</u>sto

Por favor, quiero esto. I want this, please.
por fah<u>bor</u> kee<u>yeh</u>-ro <u>eh</u>sto

… or trust the waiter's recommendation:

Por favor, quiero algo bueno. I'd like something good,
por fah<u>bor</u> kee<u>yeh</u>-ro <u>ah</u>lgo <u>bweh</u>no please.

Por favor, quiero algo bueno, I'd like something good
pero no quiero pagar that isn't too expensive,
demasiado. por fah<u>bor</u> please.
kee<u>yeh</u>-ro <u>ah</u>lgo <u>bweh</u>no, pehro
no kee<u>yeh</u>-ro pah<u>gahr</u>
dehmah<u>seeyah</u>-doh

Culture Tip

A number of Spanish dishes are known outside Spain. You surely have heard of *paella*, which is rice prepared in a pan and mixed with seafood, chicken or vegetables.

Tapas are small dishes served in bars. Among the many variations, *jamón serrano* (dried ham), *chorizo* (hot peppered salami) and *tortilla de patatas* (potato omelet) are the better known ones.

While many typical Latin American dishes, such as *tacos*, *tamales* and *quesadillas* may be familiar to you, Latin American cooking includes a wide variety of delicious foods, including excellent seafood, beef and vegetables. Try *cazuela de mariscos* (seafood in white sauce) or *ceviche* (raw fish marinated in citrus).

If you have special requests at a restaurant:

Perdón, pero tengo poco tiempo. pehr<u>don</u> <u>peh</u>ro <u>teh</u>ngo <u>po</u>ko tee<u>yehm</u>-po

Excuse me, but I don't have much time.

Perdón, pero tenemos muy poco tiempo. pehr<u>don</u> <u>peh</u>ro teh<u>neh</u>mos mwee <u>po</u>ko tee<u>yehm</u>-po

Excuse me, but we have very little time.

Por favor, quiero mucho para comer. por fah<u>bor</u> kee<u>yeh</u>-ro <u>moo</u>cho <u>pah</u>rah ko<u>mehr</u>

I would like a big portion, please.

Por favor, quiero muy poco. por fah<u>bor</u> kee<u>yeh</u>-ro mwee <u>po</u>ko

I would like just a small portion, please.

Gracias, no quiero comer nada. <u>grah</u>-seeyahs no kee<u>yeh</u>-ro ko<u>mehr</u> <u>nah</u>dah

Thank you, I don't want anything to eat.

Perdón, necesito otro …
pehr<u>don</u> nehseh<u>see</u>-to <u>o</u>tro

Excuse me, I need another …

cuchillo
koo<u>cheel</u>-yo

tenedor
tehneh<u>dor</u>

plato
<u>plah</u>to

vaso
<u>bah</u>so

If you don't get what you wanted, you could say:

Perdón, esto no es lo que yo quiero. pehr<u>don</u> <u>eh</u>sto no ehs lo keh yo kee<u>yeh</u>-ro

Excuse me, this is not what I ordered.

Yo quiero esto. yo kee<u>yeh</u>-ro <u>eh</u>sto

I would like this.

If you enjoyed your meal, show your appreciation and tell the waiter/waitress:

Esto me gusta. <u>eh</u>sto meh <u>goo</u>stah

I like this.

Esto nos gusta mucho. <u>eh</u>sto nos <u>goo</u>stah <u>moo</u>cho

We like this very much.

¡Qué bueno! keh <u>bweh</u>no

Very tasty!

¡Está muy bueno! ehs<u>tah</u> mwee <u>bweh</u>no

This is very good!

¡No está mal! no ehs<u>tah</u> mahl

Not bad!

If you would like to get an extra helping, say:

¿Podría comer más de esto, por favor? podreeah komehr mahs deh ehsto por fahbor

Could I get some more of this please?

¿Puedo comer más de esto? pwehdo komehr mahs de ehsto

Can I get some more of this?

Me gustaría comer más de esto. meh goostahree-ah komehr mahs de ehsto

I would like to eat some more of this.

Por favor, quiero un poco más. por fahbor keeyeh-ro oon poko mahs

I would like a little more please.

Perdón, esto es muy poco. pehrdon ehsto ehs mwee poko

Excuse me, this is a very small portion.

Podría comer un poco más? podreeah komehr oon poko mahs

Could I get some more?

Es muy poco. Puedo comer más? ehs mwee poko pwehdo komehr mahs

This is a very small portion. Could I get some more?

If the portion is too much for you, say:

¡Es demasiado! ehs dehmahseeyah-doh

It's too much!

¡Esto es demasiado! ehsto ehs dehmahseeyah-doh

This is too much!

No puedo comer todo esto. no pwehdo komehr todo ehsto

I can't eat all of this.

Es demasiado para uno. ehs dehmahseeyah-do pahrah oono

That is too much for one person.

Por favor, quiero uno para los dos. por fah<u>bor</u> kee<u>yeh</u>-ro <u>oo</u>no <u>pah</u>rah los dos

I would like one dish for the two of us.

If you don't like the food, you could say:

Esto no me gusta.
<u>eh</u>sto no meh <u>goo</u>stah

I don't like this.

Esto no me gusta nada.
<u>eh</u>sto no meh <u>goo</u>stah <u>nah</u>dah

I don't like this at all.

No nos gusta. no nos <u>goo</u>stah

We don't like this.

No quiero comer esto.
no kee<u>yeh</u>-ro ko<u>mehr</u> <u>eh</u>sto

I don't want to eat this.

No puedo comer esto.
no <u>pweh</u>do ko<u>mehr</u> <u>eh</u>sto

I can't eat this.

No es bueno. no ehs <u>bweh</u>no

This isn't good.

You could ask for something else instead:

¿No tiene nada mejor?
no teey<u>eh</u>neh <u>nah</u>dah meh<u>khor</u>

Don't you have anything better?

Quiero algo mejor.
kee<u>yeh</u>-ro <u>ahl</u>go meh<u>khor</u>

I want something better.

No quiero esto, quiero esto.
no kee<u>yeh</u>-ro <u>eh</u>sto kee<u>yeh</u>-ro <u>eh</u>sto

I don't want this, I want that.

Por favor, quiero menos de esto, pero más de esto.
por fah<u>bor</u> kee<u>yeh</u>-ro <u>meh</u>nos deh <u>eh</u>sto <u>peh</u>ro mahs de <u>eh</u>sto

I want a little less of this, but more of that.

When you've had enough, all you have to say is:

¡No puedo más! no _pweh_do mahs   No more! (I'm full!)

¡No podemos comer más!   We can't eat anymore!
no po_deh_mos ko_mehr_ mahs

The quality of food offers another conversation topic:

Aquí se come muy bien.   You can eat very well here.
ah_kee_ seh _ko_meh mwee bee_yehn_

Aquí se come mejor que en el…   You can eat better here
[restaurant]. ah_kee_ seh _ko_meh   than at …
meh_khor_ keh ehn ehl

Sí, y cuesta menos.   Yes, and it costs less.
see ee _kweh_stah _meh_nos

Sí, pero cuesta más.   Yes, but it costs
see _peh_ro _kweh_stah mahs   more.

Now it's time to pay up:

Por favor, quiero pagar.   I would like to pay please.
por fah_bor_ kee_yeh_-ro pah_gahr_

¿Cuánto es? _kwahn_to ehs   How much is it?

Quiero pagar esto, esto y   I would like to pay for
esto. kee_yeh_-ro pah_gahr_ _eh_sto   this and this.
_eh_sto ee _eh_sto

If you are going to pay the entire bill, you can say:

Quiero pagar todo.   I want to pay for it all.
kee_yeh_-ro pah_gahr_ _to_do

Quiero pagar por todos.　　　I want to pay for everyone.
kee<u>yeh</u>-ro pah<u>gahr</u> por <u>to</u>dos

Quiero pagar por todas. ♀　　I want to pay for everyone.
kee<u>yeh</u>-ro pah<u>gahr</u> por <u>to</u>dahs

If you enjoyed the service, give the waiter a good tip.

Gracias, esto es para usted.　Thank you, this is for you.
<u>grah</u>-seeyahs <u>eh</u>sto ehs <u>pah</u>rah
oo<u>steh</u>d

Culture Tip

Tipping practices vary widely. In Spain, tips are optional, and left only for exceptional service. Waiters in some Latin American countries expect a tip of 10% - 15%. If you're not sure whether to tip, just ask another diner.
If you want to tip the waiter but have to leave, just leave some change on the small plate that was returned with the change or the receipt.

Playing Host

If you are the host, one of your first questions will be:

¿Quieres comer algo?　　Would you like something
kee<u>yeh</u>-rehs ko<u>mehr</u> <u>ah</u>lgo　to eat? *sing. inform.*

¿Quiere beber algo?　　Would you care for a
kee<u>yeh</u>-reh beh<u>behr</u> <u>ah</u>lgo　drink? *sing. form.*

¿Qué quieres comer?　　What would you like
keh kee<u>yeh</u>-rehs ko<u>mehr</u>　to eat? *sing. inform.*

¿Qué quiere beber?　　What would you like
keh kee<u>yeh</u>-reh beh<u>behr</u>　to drink? *sing. form.*

If you want to know whether your guests are enjoying their meal ask them:

¿Te gusta? teh goostah — Do you like it? *sing. inform.*

¿Le gusta? leh goostah — Do you like it? *sing. form.*

You could also ask them whether they would like more:

¿Quieres más?
keeyeh-rehs mahs — Do you want some more? *sing. inform.*

¿Quiere un poco más?
keeyeh-reh oon poko mahs — Would you care for some more? *sing. form.*

Shopping

Here are some phrases to use when you want to go shopping:

Queremos comprar regalos.
kehrehmos komprahr rehgahlos — We would like to buy some gifts.

¿Dónde puedo comprar regalos? dondeh pwehdo komprahr rehgahlos — Where can I buy some gifts?

¿Dónde hay regalos buenos por aquí? dondeh eye rehgahlos bwehnos por ahkee — Can you get any good gifts around here?

Necesito un regalo bonito, pero no quiero pagar demasiado. nehsehseeto oon rehgahlo boneeto pehro no keeyeh-ro pahgahr dehmahseeyah-do — I am looking for a nice gift but I don't want to pay too much.

If you can't make out what something is, just ask:

¿Para qué es esto?   What is this for?
<u>pah</u>rah keh ehs <u>eh</u>sto

Language Tip

Para qué (what for) is a combination of the words *para* (for)
and *qué* (what).

¿Qué se hace con esto?   What do you do with this?
keh seh <u>ah</u>seh kon <u>eh</u>sto

¿Por favor, puedo ver esto?   May I take a look at this,
por fah<u>bor</u> <u>pweh</u>do behr <u>eh</u>sto   please?

Por favor, quiero ver esto.   I would like to take a look
por fah<u>bor</u> kee<u>yeh</u>-ro behr <u>eh</u>sto   at this, please.

If you want to buy something typical from the area, say:

Quiero comprar algo de aquí.   I would like to buy some-
kee<u>yeh</u>-ro kom<u>prahr</u> <u>ahl</u>go deh   thing from this region.
ah<u>kee</u>

¿Esto es de aquí? <u>eh</u>sto ehs   Is this from here?
deh ah<u>kee</u>

Culture Tip

Typical souvenirs from Spain are fans (*abanicos*) or castanets (*castañuelas*). Other popular souvenirs are small fig-
ures dressed up as Flamenco dancers or exquisite shells
(*conchas*) sold at seaside resorts. In Latin America, hand-
made pottery and woven blankets are popular souvenirs.

If you want to know how much something is:

¿Cuánto cuesta esto?　　　How much is this?
kwahnto kwehstah ehsto

Es mucho. ehs moocho　　　That is expensive.

Es demasiado.　　　That is too much.
ehs dehmah<u>see</u>yah-do

Quiero pagar menos por esto.　　　I want to pay less
kee<u>yeh</u>-ro pah<u>gahr</u> <u>meh</u>nos　　　for this.
por <u>eh</u>sto

Lo compro por ... [amount].　　　I'll buy it for ...
lo <u>kom</u>pro por

See page 109 for numbers.

Está bien. ehs<u>tah</u> bee<u>yeh</u>n　　　That's OK.

Culture Tip

If something appears to be overpriced, try bargaining—but only at flea markets or with street vendors. Department stores and supermarkets will not negotiate on prices.

If you want to buy something say:

Me gustaría comprar esto.　　　I want to buy this.
meh goostah<u>ree</u>-ah kom<u>prahr</u> <u>eh</u>sto

Por favor, quiero esto.　　　I'd like that, please.
por fah<u>bor</u> kee<u>yeh</u>-ro <u>eh</u>sto

Quiero esto. keeyeh-ro ehsto — I'd like this.

También quiero esto.
tahmbeeyehn keeyeh-ro ehsto — I also want this.

If there is something wrong with the item, you can say:

Está roto. ehstah roto — It is broken.

No quiero uno roto.
no keeyeh-ro oono roto — I don't want anything broken.

Es muy bonito, pero demasiado grande. ehs mwee boneeto pehro dehmahseeyah-do grahndeh — It is very nice, but it is too big.

Es muy bonito, pero cuesta demasiado. ehs mwee boneeto pehro kwehstah dehmahseeyah-do — It is very nice, but it costs too much.

¿No tiene otro?
no teeyehneh otro — Don't you have another one?

¿No tiene otro más bonito?
no teeyehneh otro mahs boneeto — Don't you have a nicer one?

¿No tiene otro menos grande?
no teeyehneh otro mehnos grahndeh — Don't you have a smaller one?

Or, if you don't like any of the products:

Gracias, pero no lo quiero.
grah-seeyahs pehro no lo keeyeh-ro — Thank you, but I don't want it.

Gracias, pero no me gusta.
grah-seeyahs pehro no meh goostah — Thank you, but I don't like it.

No lo necesito.
no lo nehseh<u>see</u>to

I don't need it.

No queremos comprar esto.
no ke<u>reh</u>mos kom<u>prahr</u> <u>eh</u>sto

We don't want to buy this.

No voy a comprar esto.
no boyee ah kom<u>prahr</u> <u>eh</u>sto

I'm not going to buy this.

No quiero comprar nada.
no kee<u>yeh</u>-ro kom<u>prahr</u> <u>nah</u>dah

I don't want to buy anything.

Sightseeing

Start out by asking about the sights in your area:

¿Qué hay que ver aquí?
keh eye keh behr ah<u>kee</u>

What can you visit here?

¿Qué hay que ver por aquí?
keh eye keh behr por ah<u>kee</u>

What sights are there in this area?

¿Qué hay que ver cerca de aquí? keh eye keh behr <u>sehr</u>kah deh ah<u>kee</u>

What is there to see around here?

¿Qué se puede ver aquí?
keh seh <u>pweh</u>deh behr ah<u>kee</u>

What can you visit here?

Next, you'll need to ask how to get there:

¿Cómo podemos ir?
<u>ko</u>mo po<u>deh</u>mos eer

How can we get there?

¿Cómo hay que ir?
<u>ko</u>mo eye keh eer

Which way do you have to go?

Hay que ir por aquí.
eye keh eer por ah<u>kee</u>

You have to go this way.

¿Cómo se va a ... [name of the sight or place]?
<u>ko</u>mo seh bah ah

How do you get to ...?

Language Tip

In Spanish the definite article usually precedes the name of a building, as in *la Plaza Mayor*: *¿Cómo se va a la Plaza Mayor?* (How do you get to the *Plaza Mayor*?). Don't forget that the masculine article *el* merges with the preposition *a* to form *al*. To ask the same question about *el Prado,* you would say: *¿Cómo se va al Prado?* (How do you get to the *Prado*?).

Names of cities, towns, etc. normally have no article. The question above would simply read: *¿Cómo se va a Segovia?* (How do you get to Segovia?).

¿... [place] está por aquí? eh<u>stah</u> por ah<u>kee</u>

Is this the way to ...?

¿... [place] está cerca de aquí?
eh<u>stah</u> <u>sehr</u>kah deh ah<u>kee</u>

Is ... around here?

Sí, está muy cerca.
see eh<u>stah</u> mwee <u>sehr</u>kah

Yes, it is very close.

¿Es aquí ... [place]? ehs ah<u>kee</u>

Is this ...?

Sí, es ... [place]. see ehs

Yes, this is ...

No, no es ... [place]. no no ehs

No, this is not ...

If you're not sure whether you are going in the right direction, you could ask:

¿Voy bien para ir a … [place]? boyee bee<u>yehn</u> <u>pah</u>rah eer ah

Is this the right way to …?

¿No vamos bien? no <u>bah</u>mos bee<u>yehn</u>

Are we going the wrong way?

No, va mal. no bah mahl

No, this isn't right.

No, tiene que ir por aquí. no tee<u>yehn</u>eh keh eer por ah<u>kee</u>

No, you have to go this way.

If you want to take public transportation or a taxi you could ask for the next bus stop or train station:

¿Dónde hay un …? <u>don</u>deh eye oon

Where is there a …?

¿Dónde puedo entrar en el …? <u>don</u>deh <u>pweh</u>deh en<u>trahr</u> ehn ehl

Where can I catch the … ?

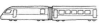

tren trehn

autobús awto<u>boos</u>

táxi <u>tah</u>see

metro <u>meh</u>tro

tranvía trahn<u>beea</u>h

When you buy your ticket, say:

Para uno, por favor.
pahrah oono por fahbor

For one person, please.

**Hasta … [place],
por favor.** ahstah … por fahbor

To …, please.

**Para dos, hasta …
[place], por favor.**
pahrah dos ahstah … por fahbor

Two tickets to ...,
please.

**Por favor, quiero ir a …
[place].** por fahbor
keeyeh-ro eer ah

I want to go to ..., please.

Once you've arrived you may want to find out whether there are any guided tours and what the entry fees are:

¿Se puede entrar?
seh pwehdeh ehntrahr

Is it possible to go inside?

¿Puedo entrar? pwehdo ehntrahr

Can I go inside?

¿Podemos entrar aquí?
podehmos ehntrahr ahkee

Can we enter here?

¿Cuesta algo entrar?
kwehstah ahlgo ehntrahr

Do you have to pay
an admission fee?

¿Cuánto cuesta entrar aquí?
kwahnto kwehstah ehntrahr ahkee

How much is it to get in?

¿Por dónde se puede entrar?
por dondeh seh pwehdeh ehntrahr

Where can you enter?

Hay que entrar por aquí.
eye keh entrahr por ahkee

You have to enter here.

¿Cuándo se puede entrar aquí?
kwahndo seh pwehdeh ehntrahr
ahkee

When can one get in here?

¿Qué hay que hacer para ver … [sight]? keh eye keh ahsehr pahrah behr

What do you have to do in order to see …?

Your guide may wish to point out interesting sights to you:

¿Lo ves? lo behs

Do you see it? *sing. inform.*

¿Lo puede ver? lo pwehdeh behr

Can you see it? *sing. form.*

Sí, lo puedo ver.
see lo pwehdo behr

Yes, I can see it.

Lo veo muy bien.
lo beho mwee beeyehn

I see it very clearly.

No lo vemos bien.
no lo behmos beeyehn

We can't see it very well.

Se puede ver mejor de aquí.
seh pwehdeh behr mehkhor deh
ahkee

One can see it better from here.

You may have questions about the sights or want to find out more about something in particular:

¿De quién es esto?
deh keeyehn ehs ehsto

Who is this by?

¿Cómo se llama esto?
komo seh yahmah ehsto

What is this called?

¿De cuándo es? deh kwahndo ehs

When was this made?

¿De qué año es? deh keh ahnyo
ehs

What year is it from?

Language Tip

The numbers you'll need to talk about years are on page 109. Years from the last century are formed with *mil novecientos* (1900), then the tens (in 87 e.g. that would be 80, *ochenta*) connected with *y* (and) to the single digits (for 87 that would be 7, *siete*). Thus, 1987 in Spanish is *mil novecientos ochenta y siete*.

The year 2000 is *dos mil. Y* is left out when there is no tens digit. Therefore, the year 2006 in Spanish is *dos mil seis*.

Going Out

If you want to find out about entertainment, ask:

¿Qué hay esta noche?
keh eye <u>eh</u>sta <u>no</u>cheh

What's going on tonight?

¿Y qué hay mañana?
ee keh eye mah<u>nyah</u>nah

And what's on tomorrow?

¿De quién es? deh kee<u>yehn</u> ehs

Who is that by?

¿Cuándo es? <u>kwahn</u>do ehs

What time will it start?

¿Es bueno? ehs <u>bweh</u>no

Is it good?

¿Podemos ir? po<u>deh</u>mos eer

Can we go there?

¿Puedo ir hoy? <u>pweh</u>do eer oyee

Can I go there today?

¿Ya no puedo ir hoy?
yah no <u>pweh</u>do eer oyee

Is it too late to go today?

¿Podemos ir mañana?
po<u>deh</u>mos eer mah<u>nyah</u>nah

Can we go tomorrow?

When you are out at an event or a party, you may want to know if somebody wants to leave:

¿Ya te vas? yah teh bahs

Are you leaving already? *sing. inform.*

¿También se va? tahmbee<u>yeh</u>n seh bah

Are you leaving too? *sing. form.*

¿Ya te quieres ir? yah teh kee<u>yeh</u>-rehs eer

Do you want to leave already? *sing. inform.*

¿Ya se quiere ir? yah seh kee<u>yeh</u>-reh eer

Do you want to leave already? *sing. form.*

¿Cuándo te vas? <u>kwahn</u>do teh bahs

When are you leaving? *sing. inform.*

¿Cuándo se va? <u>kwahn</u>do seh bah

When are you leaving? *sing. form.*

If you are the one who wants to leave or stay:

No me voy. no meh boyee

I'm not leaving.

No, no nos vamos. no no nos <u>bah</u>nos

No, we're not leaving.

Sí, me voy. see meh boyee

Yes, I am leaving.

Sí, nos vamos a la una. see nos <u>bah</u>mos ah lah <u>oo</u>nah

Yes, we're leaving at one.

Me voy a ir luego. meh boyee ah eer <u>lweh</u>go

I will leave later.

Nos vamos a ir a las dos. nos <u>bah</u>mos ah eer ah lahs dos

We will leave at two.

You may also want to know why someone is leaving:

¿Por qué te vas?
por keh teh bahs

Why are you leaving?
sing. inform.

¿Por qué se va ya?
por keh seh bah yah

Why are you going
already? *sing. form.*

Language Tip

Por qué literally translated means "for what". It is used like the English "why", not to be confused with *porque* which means "because".

If you want to say why you cannot or do not want to stay any longer:

Ya no tengo tiempo.
yah no tehngo teeyehmpo

I've got no time left.

Ya no quiero más.
yah no keeyeh-ro mahs

I've had enough.

Ya no puedo más.
yah no pwehdo mahs

I can't go on any longer.

Tengo que ir a la cama.
tehngo keh eer ah lah kahmah

I have to go to bed.

Ya es hora de ir a la cama.
yah ehs orah deh eer ah lah
kahmah

It's already time to go
to bed.

Meeting Someone

If you want to meet up with someone ask:

¿Qué haces esta tarde?　　　What are you doing
keh <u>ah</u>sehs <u>eh</u>stah <u>tahr</u>deh　　this afternoon? *sing. inform.*

Language Tip

The term *la tarde* describes an extended afternoon that starts at around 1 or 2 pm (after lunch) and extends well into the early evening, until approximately 7 pm. The time after 7 pm is called *la noche* (night).

¿Qué va a hacer mañana?　　What are doing tomorrow?
keh bah ah ah<u>sehr</u> mah<u>nyah</u>nah　*sing. form.*

¿Nos vemos luego?　　　　Will we see each other
nos <u>beh</u>mos <u>lweh</u>go　　　afterwards?

¿Nos vemos más tarde?　　Will we see each other
nos <u>beh</u>mos mahs <u>tahr</u>deh　later?

¿Nos vemos esta noche?　　Will we see each other
nos <u>beh</u>mos <u>eh</u>stah <u>no</u>cheh　tonight?

¿Nos vemos mañana?　　　Will we see each other
nos <u>beh</u>mos mah<u>nyah</u>nah　　tomorrow?

¿Nos vemos mañana por la　Will we see each other
tarde? nos <u>beh</u>mos mah<u>nyah</u>nah　tomorrow afternoon?
por lah <u>tahr</u>deh

¿Nos podemos ver luego?　　Can we see each other
nos po<u>deh</u>mos behr <u>lweh</u>go　afterwards?

¿Nos podemos ver más tarde?
nos po<u>deh</u>mos behr mahs
<u>tahr</u>deh

Can we see each other later?

¿Nos podemos ver a la una?
nos po<u>deh</u>mos behr ah lah
<u>oo</u>na

Can we see each other at one?

¿Nos podemos ver mañana a las dos? nos po<u>deh</u>mos behr mah<u>nyah</u>nah ah lahs dos

Can we see each other tomorrow at two?

Besides the time you may also wish to specify where you want to meet:

¿Nos vemos en ... ?
nos <u>beh</u>mos ehn

Shall we meet at ...?

la playa
lah <u>plah</u>-yah

la piscina
lah pees-<u>see</u>nah

el bar
ehl bahr

el restaurante
ehl rehstaw<u>rahn</u>teh

If you agree, you can say:

Sí. see

Yes.

Sí, me gustaría mucho.
see meh goosta<u>ree</u>-ah <u>moo</u>cho

Yes, I'd like that very much.

Sí, esta noche.
see <u>ehs</u>tah <u>no</u>cheh

Yes, tonight (is fine).

Sí, a las dos. see ah lahs dos

Yes, at two.

Sí, mañana a la una de la tarde. see mahnyahnah ah lah oonah deh lah tahrde

Yes, tomorrow afternoon at one.

Sí, hoy puedo. see oyee pwehdo

Yes, I can make it today.

Sí, hoy tengo tiempo. see oyee tehngo teeyehmpo

Yes, I have time today.

… or if you can't make it:

No. no

No.

No, gracias. no grah-seeyahs

No, thanks.

No, hoy no. no oyee no

No, not today.

No, hoy no puedo. no oyee no pwehdo

No, I can't make it today.

No, hoy no tengo tiempo. no oyee no tehngo teeyehmpo

No, I have no time today.

No, no quiero. no no keeyeh-ro

No, I don't want to.

If you like someone and want to move beyond friendly conversation, you can say:

Me gustas. meh goostahs

I like you.

Me gustas mucho. meh goostahs moocho

I like you very much.

If it turns into love—say it in Spanish:

Te quiero. teh keeyeh-ro

I love you.

Te quiero mucho. teh keeyeh-ro moocho

I love you very much.

Even with limited vocabulary, you can still express your love:

Te necesito para vivir.   I can't live without you.
teh neh<u>seh</u>seeto pahrah bee<u>beer</u>

Eres un regalo. <u>eh</u>rehs oon   You are a gift.
reh<u>gah</u>lo

No somos dos, somos uno.   We are not two, we are
no <u>so</u>mos dos <u>so</u>mos <u>oo</u>no   one.

And if you're ready to go a little further:

¿Quieres ver mi habitación?   Do you want to come up
kee<u>yeh</u>-rehs behr mee   to my room?
ahbeetah-<u>seeyon</u>

¿Puedo ver tu habitación?   May I come up to
<u>pweh</u>do behr too ahbeetah-   your room?
<u>seeyon</u>

If you want things to continue:

¿Nos vemos en Estados   Will we see each other
Unidos*?   in the US?
nos <u>beh</u>mos ehn ehs<u>tah</u>dos
oo<u>nee</u>dos

¿Cuándo? <u>kwahn</u>do   When?

If it's time to break it off, you can do it gently, or firmly:

---

* **Canadá** kahnah<u>dah</u>   Canada
  Gran Bretaña grahn breh<u>tah</u>nyah   Great Britain

Te quiero mucho, pero ya estoy con otro/otra.
teh kee<u>yeh</u>-ro <u>moo</u>cho <u>peh</u>ro yah ehs<u>toy</u>ee kon <u>o</u>tro/<u>o</u>trah

I like you very much, but I am with someone else.

No puedo. no <u>pweh</u>do

I can't.

Estoy aquí con ... [name].
ehs<u>toy</u>ee ah<u>kee</u> kon

I'm here with ...

No te quiero. no teh kee<u>yeh</u>-ro

I don't like/love you.

¿No ves que no quiero?
no behs keh no kee<u>yeh</u>-ro

Can't you see that I don't want to?

Problems and Emergencies

Asking for Help

Even the best of times is not free from unforeseen events. Should something happen and you need help, ask:

¿Me podrías ayudar?
meh po<u>dree</u>ahs ah-yoo<u>dahr</u>

Could you help me?
sing. inform.

¿Me podría ayudar, por favor?
meh po<u>dree</u>ah ah-yoo<u>dahr</u>
por fah<u>bor</u>

Could you help me, please? *sing. form.*

¿Me puede ayudar, por favor?
meh <u>pweh</u>deh ah-yoo<u>dahr</u>
por fah<u>bor</u>

Can you help me, please? *sing. form.*

¿Me podrías ayudar con esto, por favor? meh po<u>dree</u>ahs
ah-yoo<u>dahr</u> kon <u>eh</u>sto por
fah<u>bor</u>

Could you please help me with this? *sing. inform.*

¿Me podría ayudar a hacer esto, por favor?
meh po<u>dree</u>ah ah-yoo<u>dahr</u>
ah ah<u>sehr</u> <u>eh</u>sto por fah<u>bor</u>

Could you please help me do this? *sing. form.*

¿Me puedes hacer un favor?
meh <u>pweh</u>dehs ah<u>sehr</u> oon fah<u>bor</u>

Can you do me a favor? *sing. inform.*

¿Me podría hacer un favor?
meh po<u>dree</u>ah ah<u>sehr</u> oon fah<u>bor</u>

Could you do me a favor? *sing. form.*

¿Me haces un favor?
meh <u>ah</u>sehs oon fah<u>bor</u>

Will you do me a favor? *sing. inform.*

If any of your possessions has been lost:

Mi ... ya no está.   My ... is gone.
mee ... yah no ehs*tah*

bolso   **monedero**   **maleta**   **reloj**
*bol*so   moneh*deh*ro   mah*leh*tah   reh*lokh*

If you find something that was lost by someone else you can ask:

¿De quién es esto?   Whose is this?
deh kee*yehn* ehs *eh*sto

In case you have lost your way or don't know where you are:

Me he perdido.   meh eh pehr*dee*do   I'm lost.

Nos hemos perdido.   We're lost.
nos *eh*mos pehr*dee*do

¿Cómo puedo ir a ... [place]?   How can I get to ...?
*ko*mo *pweh*do eer ah

¿Por dónde se va a ... [place]?   Which way to ...?
por *don*deh seh bah ah

¿Dónde estoy?   *don*deh ehs*toy*ee   Where am I?

¿Dónde estamos aquí?   Where are we?
*don*deh ehs*tah*mos ah*kee*

If you need professional help ask for it by saying:

¿Dónde está la ...?   Where is the ...?
<u>don</u>deh eh<u>stah</u> lah

policía
polee<u>see</u>ah

oficina de turismo
ofee<u>see</u>nah deh too<u>rees</u>mo

Culture Tip

In case of emergency, the national help line to call in Spain is 091. The European emergency number, 112, will also put you in touch with emergency services, the doctor on call or the fire department.

Emergency phone numbers in Latin America vary by country. Check with the tourist information office, your consulate or hotel reception for the local numbers.

Illness

To tell someone that you are ill, you can say:

No estoy bien.   I am not feeling well.
no ehs<u>toy</u>ee bee<u>yehn</u>

Estoy mal. ehs<u>toy</u>ee mahl   I feel sick.

Me duele todo. meh <u>dweh</u>leh <u>to</u>do Everything hurts.

Necesito ... nehseh<u>see</u>to

I need ...

un médico
oon <u>meh</u>deeko

un dentista
oon dehn<u>tee</u>stah

una farmacia
oonah fahr<u>mah</u>seeyah

una ambulancia
oonah ahmboo<u>lahn</u>-seeyah

When you are being examined, the doctor may ask you:

¿Qué le duele?
keh leh <u>dweh</u>leh

What hurts?

¿Dónde le duele?
<u>don</u>deh leh <u>dweh</u>leh

Where does it hurt?

To answer, you can say:

Me duele aquí. meh <u>dweh</u>leh
ah<u>kee</u>

It hurts here.

Aquí me duele mucho.
ah<u>kee</u> meh <u>dweh</u>leh <u>moo</u>cho

It hurts a lot right here.

Aquí me duele más que aquí.
ah_kee_ meh dwehleh mahs keh
ah_kee_

It hurts more here than there.

Pero aquí no me duele nada.
pehro ah_kee_ no meh dwehleh
nahdah

But here it doesn't hurt at all.

If you have taken someone else to the doctor, you can point at that person's body part and say:

Le duele aquí. leh dwehleh ah_kee_   It hurts him/her there.

If you are in a lot of pain during the doctor's examination, you can say:

Aquí me duele demasiado.
ah_kee_ meh dwehleh
dehmah_seeyah_-do

It hurts very much here.

¡Cómo me duele!
ko_mo meh dwehleh

That really hurts!

Por favor, aquí no.
por fah_bor_ ah_kee_ no

Please, not here.

¡Duele demasiado!
dwehleh dehmah_seeyah_-do

It hurts too much!

If you think that you've fractured something, ask:

¿Está roto? ehs_tah_ roto   Is it broken?

¿Me he roto algo?
meh eh roto ahlgo

Have I fractured anything?

Maybe you'll get some good news from the doctor:

No tiene nada. no teeyehneh
nahdah

There's nothing wrong
with you.

No es nada. no ehs nahdah

It's nothing.

You have every reason to relax:

¡Menos mal!* mehnos mahl

You were lucky!

Things aren't too good if you're told:

Usted está muy mal.
oostehd ehstah mwee mahl

You are very ill.

Hopefully you can tell the doctor at the next visit:

Ya no me duele mucho.
yah no meh dwehleh moocho

It doesn't hurt that much
anymore.

Ya no me duele.
yah no meh dwehleh

I'm not in pain
anymore.

---

* Idiomatic expression:
  ¡Menos mal! mehnos mahl   You were lucky!

Problems

If you happen to break or damage anything, apologize by saying:

Perdón. pehr<u>don</u>   I'm sorry.

Perdón por todo.   I'm sorry for all
pehr<u>don</u> por <u>to</u>do   the trouble.

Perdón por todo esto.   I'm sorry about all that.
pehr<u>don</u> por <u>to</u>do <u>eh</u>sto

If you wish to be more specific, say:

Perdón, he roto la cama.   I'm sorry, I broke the bed.
pehr<u>don</u> eh <u>ro</u>to lah <u>kah</u>mah

Perdón, he roto …   I'm sorry, I broke the …
pehr<u>don</u> eh <u>ro</u>to

la lámpara
lah <u>lahm</u>pahrah

el televisor
ehl tehlehbee<u>sor</u>

la ducha
la <u>doo</u>chah

Perdón, he perdido …
perh<u>don</u> eh pehr<u>dee</u>do

Excuse me, I lost …

la llave
lah <u>yah</u>beh

el secador de pelo
ehl sehkah-<u>dor</u> deh <u>peh</u>lo

You may want to offer to pay for or replace the item:

¿Lo puedo pagar?
lo <u>pweh</u>do pah<u>gahr</u>

Can I pay for it?

Lo voy a pagar.
lo boyee ah pah<u>gahr</u>

I'll pay for it.

¿Podemos comprar otro?
po<u>deh</u>mos kom<u>prahr</u> <u>o</u>tro

Can we buy a
replacement?

Voy a comprar otro.
boyee ah kom<u>prahr</u> <u>o</u>tro

I'll buy a new one.

Vamos a comprar otra.
<u>bah</u>mos ah kom<u>prahr</u> <u>o</u>trah

We will buy a new one.

A

a ah to

abanico *m* ahbah<u>nee</u>ko
   fan

Adiós. ah<u>dee</u>yos
   Good-bye/Bye.

agua *f* **mineral**
   <u>ah</u>wah meeneh<u>rah</u>l
   mineral water

aletas *f/pl.* ah<u>leh</u>tahs
   flippers

algo <u>ah</u>lgo something

ambulancia *f*
   ahmboo-<u>lahn</u>seeyah
   ambulance

anillo *m* ah<u>nee</u>yo ring

año *m* <u>ah</u>nyo year

aquí ah<u>kee</u> here

ascensor *m* ahs-sehn<u>sor</u>
   elevator

autobús *m* awto<u>boos</u> bus

ayudar ahyoo<u>dahr</u> to help

B

bañera *f* bah<u>nyeh</u>rah
   bath tub

bar *m* bahr bar

beber beh<u>behr</u> to drink

bien beey<u>ehn</u> good

blusa *f* <u>bloo</u>sah blouse

bolso *m* <u>bol</u>so bag

bonito bon<u>ee</u>to nice;
   beautiful

bueno <u>bweh</u>no good

C

café *m* kah<u>feh</u> coffee

calor *m* kah<u>lor</u> warmth; heat

cama *f* <u>kah</u>mah bed

castañuelas
   f/pl. kahstah-<u>nyweh</u>-lahs
   castanets

cena *f* <u>seh</u>nah dinner

cerca <u>sehr</u>kah nearby

cerveza *f* sehr<u>beh</u>sah beer

chorizo *m* cho<u>ree</u>so hot
   pepper salami

ciudad *f* seew<u>dahd</u> city

come <u>ko</u>meh he/she eats;
   you eat [*sing. form.*]

comer ko<u>mehr</u> to eat

comida *f* ko<u>mee</u>dah
   lunch

cómo <u>ko</u>mo how

comprar kom<u>prahr</u> to buy

compro <u>kom</u>pro I buy

con kon with

concha *f* <u>kon</u>chah shell

corbata *f* kor<u>bah</u>tah necktie

costar kos<u>tahr</u> to cost

cuándo <u>kwahn</u>do when

cuánto <u>kwahn</u>to how much

cuchillo *m* koo<u>chee</u>yo knife

cuesta <u>kwehs</u>tah it costs

cuestan <u>kwehs</u>tahn
   they cost

D

de deh from; out of

demasiado dehmah-_seeyah_do too much

de nada deh _nah_dah you're welcome; it's nothing; my pleasure

dentista *m* dehn_tees_tah dentist

desayuno *m* dehsah_yoo_no breakfast

día *m* _dee_ah day

dónde _don_deh where

dormir dor_meer_ to sleep

dos dos two

ducha *f* _doo_chah shower

duele _dweh_leh it hurts

E

el the (*masculine article*)

empanada *f* ehmpah_nah_dah filled pie

en ehn in; at

ensalada *f* ehnsah_lah_dah salad

entrar ehn_trahr_ to enter

eres _eh_rehs you are [*sing. inform.*]

es ehs he/she/it is; you are [*sing. form.*]

estado ehs_tah_do was; has/have been

está ehs_tah_ he/she/it is; you are [*sing. form.*]

Está bien. ehs_tah_ beeyehn It's OK.

ésta _ehs_tah this one (*f*)

estamos ehs_tah_mos we are

estar ehs_tahr_ to be

Estados *m/pl.* **Unidos** ehs_tah_dos oo_nee_dos United States

estás ehs_tahs_ you are [*sing. inform.*]

éstas _ehs_tahs these (*f/pl.*)

éste _ehs_teh this one

esto _ehs_to this

estos _ehs_tos these (*m/pl.*)

estoy ehs_toyee_ I am

F

farmacia *f* fahr_mah_-seeyah pharmacy

favor *m* fah_bor_ favor

flamenco *m* flah_mehn_ko Andalusian dance/music

G

gafas de sol *f/pl.* _gah_fahs deh sol sun glasses

galleta *f* gah_yeh_tah cookie

gazpacho *m* gahs_pah_cho cold soup

gracias grah-seeyahs thank you

Gran Bretaña grahn brehtahnyah Great Britain

grande grahndeh big; large

gusta goostah he/she likes; you like [*sing. form.*]

gustaría goostah-reeah he/she would like

gustas goostahs you would like [*sing. inform.*]

H

habitación *f* ahbeetah-seeyon room

hace ahseh he/she/it does makes; you do make [*sing. form.*]

hacemos ahsehmos we do / make

hacer ahsehr to do / to make

haces ahsehs you do / to make [*sing. inform.*]

hago ahgo I do / make

hasta ahstah until

hay ayee there is

hay que ayee keh one has to

he eh I have

helado *m* ehlahdo ice-cream

hemos ehmos we have

hola olah hello

hoy oyee today

I

iglesia *f* eegleh-seeyah church

ir eer to go

J

jamón serrano *m* khahmon sehrrahno air-dried country ham

L

la the *(feminine article)*

lámpara *f* lahmpahrah lamp

las lahs the *(feminine plural article)*

lavabo *m* lahbahbo sink

le leh him/her/it

llave *f* yahbeh key

lo lo to him/her/it

los los the *(masculine plural article)*

luego lwehgo later; afterwards

M

mal mahl bad; poorly

maleta *f* mahl<u>eh</u>tah suitcase

mañana mah-<u>nyah</u>nah tomorrow

mañana *f* mah-<u>nyah</u>nah morning

más mahs more

me meh me; to me

me llamo meh <u>yah</u>mo I'm called (my name is)

médico *m* <u>meh</u>deeko doctor

mejor meh<u>khor</u> better

menos <u>meh</u>nos less

¡Menos mal! <u>meh</u>nos mahl You were lucky!

metro *m* <u>meh</u>tro subway

mi mee mine

monedero *m* moneh<u>deh</u>ro purse

mucho <u>moo</u>cho much

muy mwee very

N

nada <u>nah</u>dah nothing

necesitamos nehsehsee-<u>tah</u>mos we need

necesitar nehsehsee-<u>tahr</u> to need

necesito nehseh-<u>see</u>to I need

nevera *f* neh<u>beh</u>rah refrigerator

no no no; not

noche *f* <u>no</u>cheh night

nos nos us

O

oficina de turismo *f* ohfee<u>see</u>-nah deh too<u>rees</u>mo tourist office

otro <u>o</u>tro another; one more

P

paella *f* pa<u>eh</u>yah Spanish rice dish

pagar pah<u>gahr</u> to pay

para <u>pah</u>rah for; in order to

para qué <u>pah</u>rah keh what for

perdido pehr<u>dee</u>do lost; confused

Perdón. pehr<u>don</u> Excuse me.

pero <u>peh</u>ro but

piscina *f* pees-<u>see</u>nah swimming pool

plato *m* <u>plah</u>to plate

playa *f* <u>plah</u>yah beach

poco <u>po</u>ko little

podemos podehmos
we can

poder podehr to be able;
to be allowed to

podría podreeah
he/she/it could; you could
[*sing. form.*]

podrías podreeahs
you could [*sing. inform.*]

policía f poleesee-ah
police

por por for; while

por favor por fahbor please

por qué por keh why

puede pwehdeh he/she can;
you can [*sing. form.*]

puedes pwehdehs you can
[*sing. inform.*]

puedo pwehdo I can

Q

que keh as; what; this/that;
which

qué keh what?, which?
[*in question*];
How ...! [*in exclamation*]

queremos kehrehmos
we want

querer kehrehr to want; to
wish; to love

quién keeyehn who

quiere keeyehreh he/she/it
wants; he/she/it loves; you
want; you love [*sing. form.*]

quieres keeyehrehs you
want; you love
[*sing. inform.*]

quiero keeyehro I want; I
love

R

regalo m rehgahlo gift

reloj m rehlokh watch

restaurante m rehstaw-rahn-
teh restaurant

roto roto broken; torn; fractured

S

se seh oneself; someone

se llama seh yahmah
he/she/it is called; you are
called [*sing. form.*]

secador de pelo m
sehkahdor deh pehlo
hairdryer

ser sehr to be

sí see yes

siesta f seeyehstah
midday break; nap

sombrero m sombrehro hat

somos somos we are

son son they are

sopa *f* sopah soup

soy soyee I am

su soo his/hers/its; theirs; yours [*sing., form.*]

T

también tahmbeeyehn also

tapas *f/pl.* tahpahs small appetizers served in bars

tarde tahrdeh late

tarde *f* tahrdeh afternoon; evening

táxi *m* tahksee taxi

te teh you

te llamas teh yahmahs you are called [*sing. inform.*]

teléfono *m* tehlehfono telephone

televisor *m* tehleh-beesor television

tenedor *m* tehnehdor fork

tenemos tehnehmos we have

tener tehnehr to have

tener que tehnehr keh must; to have to

tengo tehngo I have

tiempo *m* teeyehmpo time; weather

tiene teeyehneh he/she/it has; you have [*sing. form.*]

tienes teeyehnehs you have [*sing. inform.*]

todo todo everything; all

¡Todo lo mejor! todo lo mehkhor All the best!

tortilla de patatas *f* torteeyah deh pahtahtahs potato omelet

tranvía *m* trahnbeeah tramcar

tren *m* trehn train

tu too yours [*sing. inform.*]

U

un *m* oon one

una *f* oonah one

uno oono one

usted oostehd you [*sing. form.*]

V

va bah he/she/it goes; you go [*sing. form.*]

vamos bahmos we go

vas bahs you go [*sing. inform.*]

vaso *m* bahso glass

vemos behmos we see

ventilador *m* behntee-lah<u>dor</u>
  fan

veo <u>beh</u>o I see

ver behr to see; to meet

ves behs you see
  [*sing. inform.*]

vestido *m* behs<u>teedo</u> dress

vino *m* <u>bee</u>no wine

vive <u>bee</u>beh he/she/it lives;
  you live [*sing. form.*]

vives <u>bee</u>behs you live
  [*sing. inform.*]

vivimos bee<u>bee</u>mos we live

vivir bee<u>beer</u> to live

vivo <u>bee</u>bo I live

voy boyee I go

W

wáter *m* <u>bah</u>tehr toilet

Y

y ee and

ya yah already

yo yo I

Numbers

0 **cero** sehro	1 **uno** <u>oo</u>no	2 **dos** dos	3 **tres** trehs
4 **cuatro** <u>kwah</u>tro	5 **cinco** <u>seen</u>ko	6 **seis** seyees	7 **siete** see<u>yeh</u>teh
8 **ocho** <u>o</u>cho	9 **nueve** <u>nweh</u>beh	10 **diez** dee<u>yehs</u>	11 **once** <u>on</u>seh
12 **doce** <u>do</u>seh	13 **trece** <u>treh</u>seh	14 **catorce** kah<u>tor</u>seh	15 **quince** <u>keen</u>seh
16 **dieciséis** deeyehsee-<u>seyees</u>	17 **diecisiete** deeyehsee- see<u>yeh</u>te	18 **dieciocho** deeyehsee-<u>o</u>cho	19 **diecinueve** deeyehsee- <u>nweh</u>beh
20 **veinte** <u>beyeen</u>teh	21 **veintiuno** beyeentee- <u>oo</u>no	22 **veintidos** beyeente- <u>dos</u>	30 **treinta** treyeentah
31 **treinta y uno** treyeentah ee <u>oo</u>no	40 **cuarenta** kwah<u>rehn</u>- tah	41 **cuarenta y uno** kwah<u>rehn</u>tah ee <u>oo</u>no	50 **cincuenta** seenk- <u>wehn</u>tah
51 **cincuenta y uno** seenk<u>wehn</u>tah ee <u>oo</u>no	60 **sesenta** seh<u>sehn</u>tah	61 **sesenta y uno** seh<u>sehn</u>tah ee <u>oo</u>no	70 **setenta** seh<u>tehn</u>tah
71 **setenta y uno** seh<u>tehn</u>tah ee <u>oo</u>no	80 **ochenta** o<u>chehn</u>tah	81 **ochenta y uno** o<u>chehn</u>tah ee <u>oo</u>no	90 **noventa** no<u>behn</u>tah

91	100	101
noventa y uno	**cien**	**ciento uno**
no<u>behn</u>tah ee <u>oo</u>no	see<u>yehn</u>	see<u>yehn</u>to <u>oo</u>no

200	1000	2000
doscientos	**mil**	**dos mil**
dos-<u>seeyehn</u>tos	meel	dos meel

679
seiscientos setenta y nueve
seyees-<u>seeyehn</u>tos seh<u>tehn</u>tah ee <u>nweh</u>beh

Language Tip

Numbers over 20 that end in *-uno* will <u>always</u> end in *-ún* if positioned before a noun: *veintiún regalos* (21 presents), *veintiún habitaciones* (21 rooms).

Even if numbers such as *treinta y uno* (31) or *cuarenta y uno* (41) are written as three separate words, they are spoken as one word without a pause in between.

Days of the Week

Monday	Tuesday	Wednesday
lunes	**martes**	**miércoles**
loonehs	mahrtehs	meeyehrkolehs

Thursday	Friday	Saturday
jueves	**viernes**	**sábado**
khwehbehs	beeyehrnehs	sahbahdo

Sunday
domingo
domeengo

Language Tip

In Spanish the days of the week all take the masculine article *el*.